Foreign Direct Investment (FDI) and Global Financial Crisis

Foreign Direct Investment (FDI)

and

Global Financial Crisis

Edited by

Rais Ahmad

Formerly Professor, Centre for Management Studies,
Jamia Millia Islamia, New Delhi

New Century Publications
New Delhi, India

NEW CENTURY PUBLICATIONS
4800/24, Bharat Ram Road,
Ansari Road, Daryaganj,
New Delhi – 110 002 (India)

Tel.: 011-2324 7798, 4358 7398, 6539 6605
Fax: 011-4101 7798
E-mail: indiatax@vsnl.com • info@newcenturypublications.com
www.newcenturypublications.com

Editorial office:
LG–7, Aakarshan Bhawan,
4754-57/23, Ansari Road, Daryaganj,
New Delhi – 110 002

Tel.: 011-4356 0919

First Published: **2013**

ISBN: **978-81-7708-338-5**

Published by New Century Publications and printed at Salasar Imaging Systems, New Delhi.

Designs: Patch Creative Unit, New Delhi.

PRINTED IN INDIA

Dedicated to

Professor Irfan Habib

Professor Emeritus,
Department of History,
Aligarh Muslim University, Aligarh

FOREWORD

Foreign direct investment can play a significant role as a supplement to domestic savings and investment, particularly in developing countries, which are generally characterized by low rates of savings and investment. It is considered to be the lifeblood for economic development. In recognition of the important role of foreign direct investment (FDI), the Government of India initiated a slew of economic and financial reforms in 1991. Since the liberalization of the Indian economy, FDI inflows have greatly increased. There is considerable evidence that FDI can affect growth and development by complementing domestic investment and by facilitating trade and transfer of knowledge and technology. Foreign direct investment (FDI) or foreign investment refers to the net inflows of investment to acquire a lasting management interest (10 percent or more of voting stock) in an enterprise operating in an economy other than that of the investor.

India has emerged as the second most attractive destination for FDI after China and ahead of the US, Russia and Brazil. Between 1991 and 2005, investments of 10 countries accounted for 71 percent of FDI, the main investor countries being the US, the Netherlands, Japan, and the United Kingdom. US was one of the largest foreign direct investors in India, however from 2005-2010 Mauritius took the lead followed by Singapore, the US and the UK among the leading sources of FDI. India is ranked second in the world in terms of manufacturing capability. As per the data available, sectors which have attracted higher inflows are services, telecommunication, construction activities and computer software and hardware. The United Nations Conference on Trade and Development (UNCTAD) has quoted recently in its World Investment Report that India would emerge as the third largest foreign direct investment (FDI) destination for the three-year period ending 2012. India remained in the list of top ten countries in 2009 to have the highest FDI in the world. In 2009, the country received FDI worth $34.6 billion, while the outward FDI was $14.9 billion, the Report said. The FDI Inflows to service sector has helped the development of several industries in the service sector of the Indian Economy, such as telecommunication, financial and non-financial services, hotel and tourism, and many others. FDI stocks and production are equally reinforcing the domestic manufacturing sector.

FDI in India is on the increase but the country has not experienced a rapid growth of FDI inflow. Since the last two decades, the FDI concept has come to play an important role in the economic development of large number of countries in the world. Therefore, it is now widely recognized that FDI can offer important advantages for the recipient economy in addition to capital inflows. FDI can lead to transfer of technology and know-how, improve access to international markets and spur competition. Moreover, with an expected downturn in the global flows of the FDI in the coming years, the competition among various locations of FDI is likely to intensify further. Countries are likely to step up their efforts to attract FDI flows, for example, further efforts to liberalize FDI entry into host economies by opening new sectors to foreign investment and more proactive investment promotion measures. The increased importance of FDI for economic development, coupled with greater competition between locations, has made investment promotion a growing activity for the government not only in developed countries, but also in developing countries. Today, there are very few countries they do not have an institution to deal with the promotion of inward investment. In fact, many countries are not maintaining such institutions on a national level, but they may have it at sub-national level.

It is expected that the present book will be highly useful for policy makers, researchers and academicians.

Professor Z.U. Khairoowala
Chairman,
Department of Commerce,
Aligarh Muslim University,
Aligarh

About the Book

Foreign investment is a subject of topical interest. Countries of the world, particularly developing economies, are vying with each other to attract foreign capital to boost their domestic rates of investment and also to acquire new technology and managerial skills. Intense competition is taking place among the fund-starved less developed countries to lure foreign investors by offering repatriation facilities, tax concessions and other incentives. However, foreign investment is not an unmixed blessing. Governments in developing countries have to be very careful while deciding the magnitude, pattern and conditions of private foreign investment.

In India, foreign investment policies in the post-reforms period have emphasised greater encouragement and mobilisation of non-debt creating private inflows for reducing reliance on debt flows. Progressively, liberal policies have led to increasing inflows of foreign investment in the country.

Recently, the Government of India cleared the most-awaited reform measure, allowing foreign direct investment (FDI) in multi-brand retail up to 51 percent, paving the way for international multi-brand retailers to set up business in India. This apart, liberalized FDI norms for aviation, broadcasting, insurance and pension sectors have also been cleared.

This book contains 8 scholarly papers, authored by experts in the field, which provide analytical account of foreign direct investment (FDI) in India in the context of ongoing global financial crisis.

Editor's Profile

Dr. Rais Ahmad is formerly Head and Associate Professor, Department of Agricultural Economics and Business Management, Aligarh Muslim University (AMU), Aligarh. He is also ex-Professor of the Centre for Management Studies, Jamia Millia Islamia, New Delhi.

He received his M.Com., M.Phil. and Ph.D. degrees from AMU. He has recently completed a major research project on micro finance and self-help groups (SHGs) financed by University Grants Commission (UGC), New Delhi. He has to his credit 8 books and several research papers published in professional journals.

Contents

Contributors

Pramila Singh Research Scholar, V.S.S.D. College, Nawabganj, Kanpur.

D.C. Gupta Reader, Department of Commerce, V.S.S.D. College, Nawabganj, Kanpur.

D. Boopath Associate Professor, Department of Mass Communication and Journalism, P.S.G. College of Arts and Science, Coimbatore.

Rajesh C. Jampala Professor and Head, Department of Commerce and Business Administration, P.B. Siddhartha College of Arts and Science, Siddhartha Nagar, Vijayawada.

P. Adi Lakshmi Professor and Head, Department of Business Administration, P.V.P. Siddhartha Institute of Technology, Kanuru, Vijayawada.

Srinivasa Rao Dokku Assistant Professor, P.V.P. Siddhartha Institute of Technology, Kanuru, Vijayawada.

P. Srinivasan Ph.D. Scholar, Department of Economics, Pondicherry University, School of Management, Puducherry.

M. Kalaivani Ph.D. Scholar, Department of Economics, Periyar University, Salem, Tamil Nadu.

P. Ibrahim Senior Professor, Department of Economics, Pondicherry University, School of Management, Puducherry.

Amrik Singh Sudan Post-graduate Department of Commerce, University of Jammu, Jammu.

Rais Ahmad   Department of Agricultural Economics and
                 Business Management, Aligarh Muslim
                 University, Aligarh.

Radha Gupta Department of Management, Baba Ghulam
                 Shah Badshah University, Rajouri, (J&K).

Anil Suresh Assistant Professor of Commerce,
                 Madras Christian College, Chennai.

R. Narayanan Assistant Professor of Business Administration,
                 Directorate of Distance Education,
                 Annamalai University, Annamalainagar.

Preface

Investment in a country by individuals and organisations from other countries is an important aspect of international finance. This flow of international finance may take the form of direct investment (creation of productive facilities) or portfolio investment (acquisition of securities).

FDI is the outcome of the mutual interests of multinational firms and host countries. The essence of FDI is the transmission to the host country of a package of capital, managerial, skill and technical knowledge. FDI is generally a form of long-term international capital movement, made for the purpose of productive activity and accompanied by the intention of managerial control or participation in the management of a foreign firm.

In India, FDI means investment by non-resident entity/person resident outside India in the capital of an Indian company under Schedule 1 of Foreign Exchange Management (Transfer or Issue of Security by a Person Resident Outside India) Regulations, 2000.

FDI is usually contrasted with portfolio investment which does not seek management control, but is motivated by profit. Portfolio investment occurs when individual investors invest, mostly through stockbrokers, in stocks of foreign companies in foreign land in search of profit opportunities.

However, the distinction between FDI and portfolio investment is not watertight because sometimes FDI policy and portfolio investment are intertwined.

FDI is widely considered an essential element for achieving sustainable development. Even former critics of MNCs expect FDI to provide a stronger stimulus to income growth in host countries than other types of capital inflows. Developing countries are strongly advised to rely primarily on FDI, in order to supplement national savings by capital inflows and promote economic development.

FDI flows are usually preferred over other forms of

external finance because they are non-debt creating, non-volatile and their returns depend on the performance of the projects financed by the investors. FDI also facilitates international trade and transfer of knowledge, skills and technology. In a world of increased competition and rapid technological change, their complimentary and catalytic role can be very valuable.

In contrast to foreign lenders and portfolio investors, foreign direct investors typically have a long-term perspective when engaging in a host country. Hence, FDI inflows are less volatile and easier to sustain at times of crisis. While debt inflows may finance consumption rather than investment in the host country, FDI is more likely to be used productively.

FDI is expected to have relatively strong effects on economic growth, as FDI provides for more than just capital. FDI offers access to internationally available technologies and management know-how, and may render it easier to penetrate world markets.

The risk-sharing properties of FDI are undisputed. This suggests that FDI is the appropriate form of external financing for developing countries, which have less capacity than highly developed economies to absorb external shocks. Likewise, the evidence supports the predominant view that FDI is more stable than other types of capital inflows.

However, positive growth effects of FDI cannot be taken for granted. The ambiguous, and sometimes contradictory, empirical findings indicate that FDI must no longer be considered to be a homogenous and universally applicable phenomenon in order to improve our understanding of the growth impact of FDI. In the ultimate analysis, it all depends on time-varying and location-specific factors whether FDI and growth are positively correlated or not. For example, opening up early to FDI inflows, combined with close integration into world trade, seems to have strengthened the FDI/growth nexus. The good news for small and less advanced economies is that they can benefit from positive growth effects of FDI as much as large and more advanced developing countries.

Prior to reforms, foreign investment in India was allowed generally in areas of hi-tech, sophisticated technologies and substantial exports. The normal ceiling for foreign investment was 40 percent of the total equity capital, but a higher percentage of foreign equity was considered in priority industries if the technology was sophisticated and not available in the country, or if the venture was largely export-oriented.

Since 1991, the Government of India has embarked on a liberalisation and economic reforms programme with a view to bring about rapid and substantial economic growth and move towards globalisation of the economy. The new policies have substantially relaxed restrictions on foreign investment, industrial licensing and foreign exchange. Capital market has been opened to foreign investment and banking sector controls have been eased.

I place on record my deep sense of gratitude to the contributors to this volume. Their scholarly analysis of global financial crisis and FDI policy of India will provide deep insights into this topical subject.

Aligarh   **Rais Ahmad**
October 2012

1

India's Foreign Capital Policy Since 1947

Pramila Singh and D.C. Gupta

Soon after Independence in 1947, the policy on foreign capital was enunciated in a Statement made in Parliament by Prime Minister Jawaharlal Nehru in November 1949. First Five Year Plan (1951-56) clearly enunciated Government's policy regarding foreign capital by stating, "In securing rapid industrial development under present conditions, foreign capital has an important part to play. A free flow of foreign capital should be welcome because it will ensure the supply of capital goods and of technical know-how. The Government's policy in this regard gives the following assurances to foreign capital: (a) there will be no discrimination between foreign and Indian undertakings in the application of general industrial policy, (b) reasonable facilities will be given for the remittance of profits and repatriation of capital, consistently with the foreign exchange position of the country, and (c) in the event of nationalisation fair and equitable compensation would be paid." [1]

Phase 1 (1948 to 1966): Cautious Welcome
India lacked a policy of its own on foreign capital before Independence 'because' it derived its faith in total *laissez faire* from the British government. Resultantly, foreign enterprises found it convenient to export products to India and were justified by local circumstances to set-up branches or wholly owned subsidiaries. Local entrepreneurs, which did not have many prospects for obtaining foreign collaboration, set-up industrial units without foreign collaborators as in the case of

cotton textiles, cement and paper or obtained the services of foreign consultants as in the case of steel (Tata Iron and Steel Company).

The advent of Independence brought into focus the various issues involved in the import of foreign capital and expertise into the country, and the need for defining a policy with respect to foreign investment. The new independent government had specific views on industrialization and role of foreign capital. This was reflected in the first policy document, Industrial Policy Resolution of 1948.

The Industrial Policy Resolution of 1948 recognized that participation of foreign capital and enterprise, particularly as regards industrial techniques and knowledge would be of value for the rapid industrialization of the country. However, it was necessary that the conditions under which foreign capital could participate in Indian industry should be carefully regulated in national interest. As a rule, the major interest in ownership and effective control would normally be in Indian hands though provision was made for special cases in a manner calculated to serve the national interest.

In the mid-1950s when industrialization got underway foreign capital ventured into India primarily with technical collaboration. However, the foreign exchange crisis of 1958 marked a change in foreign collaboration in India in two ways: (i) foreign enterprise began to take equity participation more frequently, (ii) more of technical collaborations started to accept equity participation in lieu of royalties and fees. After 1958, Indian entrepreneurs were given provisional licenses required to secure part or all of the foreign exchange by way of foreign investment. The government extended the AID Investment Guarantee Program to cover American private investment in India. It gave a number of tax concessions to foreign enterprise. The licensing procedure was streamlined to avoid delays in approvals of foreign collaboration. Double taxation avoidance agreements with Finland, France, U.S.A., Pakistan, Ceylon, Sweden, Norway, Denmark, Japan and West

Germany were signed.

In 1963-64, the Government of India decided to give 'letters of intent' to foreign companies to proceed with their capital projects, instead of making the foreign company find an Indian partner and then giving the 'letter of intent' to the Indian partner. It was also decided to make the services of IDBI available for rupee finance required by such undertakings.

The Finance Act, 1965 made provision for certain additional tax concessions. The interest accruing in a Non-Resident Account on money transferred from abroad through recognized banking channels and deposited in any bank in India was exempted from tax. Also the tax exemption limit of 5 years allowed in respect of salaries of foreign technicians was extended to 7 years. Tax rates on income assessable in India of non-residents were brought down at par with those applicable to income of residents. The rate or deduction of tax at source from non-residents income was also lowered. The Act further provided for the refund of capital gains tax arising from the transfer of shares held by non-resident in an Indian company, provided the sale proceeds were invested in India.

In May 1966, the government decided that investments by NRIs would be allowed without any limit in public limited industrial concerns in India. In private limited industrial concerns with a minimum issued and paid up capital of ₹ 10 lakh, their share would be allowed up to 49 percent. In special cases it would be increased to 51 percent or even more, provided resident Indian participation would go up to 49 percent within a period of say 5 years. But they would not be allowed to invest in proprietorship/partnership and dividends would not be allowed to be repatriated.

Phase II (1967-1979): Selective/Restrictive Approach

Under the new industrial licensing policy, announced in February, 1970 the larger industrial houses and foreign enterprises were permitted to setup industries in the 'core' and the 'heavy investments' sectors except industries reserved for the Public Sector. By notification dated July 25, 1970, they established undertakings and expanded production in industries in other sectors provided they undertook specific export commitments. However, in order to prevent a serious draft on their reserves, the remittance facilities in respect of dividends declared by 100 percent foreign owned companies were subject to some terms.

In 1972-73, though the Government Policy towards foreign investment continued to attract foreign investment in India, the policy became highly selective. Foreign exchange Regulation Act was amended in 1973, to regulate the entry of foreign capital in the form of branches, non-resident Indians investment and employment of foreigners in India. As per the amended rules all branches of foreign companies in India and Indian Joint Stock Companies in which non-resident interest was more than 40 percent were expected to bring down their non-resident share holdings to 40 percent within a period of 2 years.

However, basic and core industries, export-oriented industry or industries engaged in manufacturing activities needing sophisticated technology or tea plantation industry were allowed to carry on business with non-resident interest up to 74 percent. Such companies were also exempted from taking permission from RBI to carry on business provided they did not exceed the licensed capacity and undertook no expansion or diversification of activities. Foreign shipping companies were given permission to carry on business in India in October 1974.

With a view to encourage investment by non-resident Indians, in October 1975, the government decided to permit non-resident Indians and persons of Indian origin to invest in the equity capital of permitted industries up to a maximum of 20 percent of new issues of capital of new Industries. Such investments were made by remittances from abroad through approved banking channels or out of funds held in non-resident (external) account. The investment could be in addition to any foreign equity investment that could be permitted by the government in the company concerned.

In October 1976, the scheme under which non-resident Indians were allowed to start industrial units in India by bringing in imported machinery was liberalized to permit equity investment up to 74 percent without any minimum limit in a number of priority sector industries. The permission was also granted for investment in other industries provided the investor undertook to export 60 percent of the output (75 percent in case of industries reserved for small-scale sector). The scheme was applicable only to new units and to existing industrial undertaking seeking expansion and diversification. Capital invested under the scheme was eligible for repatriation after the unit had gone into commercial production subject to adherence to export obligation.

A statement on Industrial Policy was presented by the Government to Parliament on December 23, 1977. Under this statement foreign investment and acquisition of technology necessary for India's industrial development could be allowed where they were in national interest and on terms determined by the government. As a rule majority interest in ownership and effective control could he in Indian hands except in highly export-oriented and sophisticated technology areas and 100 percent export-oriented areas. Where foreign investments had been approved, there could he complete freedom of remittance of profits, royalties, dividends and repatriation of capital subject to the usual regulations. The government had made it clear that while it would strictly enforce the provisions of FERA, the companies which diluted their non-resident holdings to less than 40 percent would be treated at par with Indian companies except in cases specifically notified. Their future expansion would be guided by the same principles as those applicable to Indian companies.

In terms of the said policy the government prepared a revised illustrative list of industries where no foreign collaboration, technical or financial was considered necessary due to development of indigenous technology.

Phase III (1980-1990): Partial Liberalization

In order to tap the resources tram oil exporting developing countries, the government revised the foreign investment policy in October 1980 so that investment proposals from these countries need not be associated with transfer of technology and that such investment could be of a portfolio nature. However, a ban was imposed by the government on financial and technical collaboration in 22 categories of industries such as cement, paper and consumer goods and several other industries where indigenous technology was sufficiently developed with the country.

In 1982-83, the government liberalized facilities with regard to bank deposits and investments in equity shares of the corporate sector. These facilities were further liberalized in July-August, 1982 to cover preference shares and debentures issued by Indian companies. The Reserve Bank of India also simplified the exchange control procedural formalities to facilitate such investments. The government also decided to borrow from international capital markets to the extent that the availability of the low cost unilateral and bilateral resources fell short of the requirement of external resources. In line with this policy, Indian enterprises both public and private companies had been selectively permitted to raise funds abroad. However, the facilities available for deposits in non-resident account and in shares of Indian companies were confined to non-resident individuals of Indian nationality or origin. Liberalized facilities were extended to overseas companies, partnership firms, trusts, societies and other corporate bodies in which at least 60 percent of the ownership/beneficial interest was vested in non-resident individuals of Indian nationality or origin.

It was specified that in case of investment, with repetriability, by non-residents Indians and overseas corporate bodies can make portfolio investment through stock exchanges in India in equity/preference shares and convertible/non-convertible debentures without any limit on the quantum or value. They could also invest in the new issues of public or private limited companies in any business activity (except real estate business) up to 100 percent of the issued capital without any obligation to associate resident Indian participation in the equity capital at any time. Payment for purchases either through stock exchanges or for direct investment in new issues could be made by the eligible investor either: (a) by fresh remittances from abroad or (b) out of the funds held in non-resident external accounts designated in rupees or in foreign currencies and ordinary non-resident accounts.

In 1983-84, the government provided incentives in the form of: (i) taxation of investment income derived by a non-resident of Indian nationality or Indian origin from the specified investments and long-term capital gains arising out of transfer of these assets at a flat rate of 20 percent plus surcharge of 12½ percent of such income tax, (ii) exemption of long-term capital gains arising from the transfer of any foreign exchange asset, (iii) exemption from wealth tax of the value of foreign exchange assets acquired and held by non-resident, (iv) Exemption from gift tax of gifts of foreign exchange assets by non-residents Indian to their relatives in India, and (v) additional interest of 1 percent on investments by NRIs in the 6-year NSCs would be paid provided subscription for these certificates were received in foreign exchange.

In May 1983, relaxations granted to NRIs investment were subjected to a specific limit. An overall ceiling of: (a) 5 percent of the value of the total paid up equity of the company concerned, and (b) 5 percent of the total paid up value of each series of convertible debentures was fixed on purchases of equity stock exchanges on repatriation and non-repatriation basis together.

In 1985-86, the government abolished the estate duty, which was considered as one of the major hurdles in the way of inward remittances to India by non-residents of Indian nationality or origin. The surcharge on income tax was also abolished bringing down effective rate of tax on NRI income from 22.5 percent to 20 percent.

During 1986-87, the government permitted NRIs to subscribe to the Memorandum and Articles of Association of a new company and take up their share up to the face value of ₹ 10,000 for the purpose of its incorporation. It also permitted Indian companies with more than 40 percent non-resident interest to acquire immovable properties in India. Further, NRIs were allowed to invest: (i) up to 100 percent of the equity capital in sick industrial units, (ii) in new issues of Indian shipping companies under the 40 percent scheme, and (iii) in diagnostic centres in India under 40 percent or 74 percent scheme.

The government also decided to remove the quantitative ceiling of ₹ 40 lakh for making investment in India by NRIs in private limited companies under the 40 percent scheme. With a view to augmenting the inflows, the Foreign Currency (NR) Account scheme was extended to cover DM and Yen and a differential interest rate scheme was introduced with effect from August 1, 1988.

Phase IV (1991-2001): Open Door Policy

As a part of the structural adjustment policies introduced in the Indian economy by the government of India since July 1991, policies relating to foreign financial participation in Indian companies and those relating to foreign technology agreements had also undergone a radical change. Three tiers for approving proposals for foreign direct investment in the country were introduced:

1. The Reserve Banks' automatic approval system.
2. Secretariat for Industrial Approvals for considering proposals within the general.
3. Foreign Investment Promotion Board specially created to invite, negotiate and facilitate substantial investment by

international companies that would provide access to high technology and work markets.

In case of investment with benefits of repatriation of capital and income NRIs and OCBs were permitted to make investment in shares and debentures through stock exchanges up to 1 percent of the paid up value of equity/preferences and convertible debentures of the company. No limit either on quantum or value was stipulated with regard to purchases of non-convertible debentures. With the benefit of repatriation, investment in new issues of non-convertible debentures was allowed without any monetary limit.

However, in case of new issue of shares and convertible debentures through prospectuses, they could invest up to 10 percent of the new capital raised with repatriation benefit. They could also invest in the capital raised other than through prospectus up to 40 percent of the new issues of shares or convertible debentures of any company (public or private) subject to a quantitative ceiling of ₹ 40 lakh. The liberalized facility of direct investment by NRIs was confined only to capital raised by companies for setting up new industrial projects or for expansion/diversification of existing industrial undertaking. However, with the abolition of the list of industries which were not open for direct investment by non-residents and with the addition of the hotel industry, the scope for investment by NRIs had been widened.

NRIs and OCBs had also been permitted to invest in 12 percent, 6 year National Saving Certificates (NSCs) and it was exempted from wealth, income and gift taxes. The Government of India permitted equity share holding of foreign investors to be maintained at a level of 51 percent or below. It was the same level of foreign equity, which the foreign majority companies had been allowed under the FERA even when there was a likelihood of its reduction.

As per the new policy, fully owned foreign enterprises were allowed to set-up giant power projects without the requirement to balance dividend payments with export earnings. FERA companies (those having more than 40 percent foreign equity) were treated at par with Indian companies. FERA companies were also given the facility of 51 percent equity. Companies could use foreign brand names and trademarks on goods for sale within the country. Except for 22 industries in the consumer goods sector, the earlier stipulation that dividend remittances of companies receiving approval under the foreign equity up to 51 percent scheme must be balanced by export earnings over a period of 7 years was scrapped in respect of all foreign direct investment including NRIs and OCBs.

The foreign private equity in oil refineries was limited at 26 percent. Foreign Institutional Investors (FIIs) were permitted to invest in all the securities traded on primary and secondary markets. Portfolio investments in primary and secondary markets were subjected to a ceiling of 24 percent of issued share capital for the total holdings of all registered FIIs, in any company. The holding of a single FII in any company was subjected to a ceiling of 5 percent of total issued capital. NRIs/OCBs could invest with full repatriation benefits up to 100 percent in high priority industries and export- oriented industries and sick units, and power generation. In the context of such revisions, the earlier 74 percent scheme has been discontinued.

During 1993-94, the tax rate on short-term capital gains were reduced from 75 percent to 30 percent. An Electronic Hardware Technology Park (EHTP) scheme was set-up to allow 100 percent equity participation, duty free import of capital goods and a tax holiday. The ceiling on foreign equity participation in Indian companies engaged in mining activity was hiked to 50 percent. Disinvestment by foreign investors was permitted on a near automatic basis on stock exchanges in India through a registered merchant banker or a stock broker or on private basis. NRIs (but not OCBs) were allowed to invest up to 100 percent on non-repatriation basis in any partnership/sole proprietorship or in private/public limited companies (except in agricultural or plantation activities) without RBI's approval.

In 1994-95, the Reserve Bank of India decided to allow NRIs/OCBs and also FIIs, to invest in all activities except agriculture and plantation activities on a repatriation basis. The aggregate allocation of shares/convertible debentures qualifying for repatriation benefits to such non-residing investors could not exceed 24 percent of the new issue. However, FIIs were not eligible to make investment in unlisted/private limited companies under the scheme. The funds for such investment could be received by way of remittance from abroad through normal banking channels or by debit to NRI/FCNR Account of the non-resident investor. A general permission was also granted to NRIs/OCBs to-purchase the shares on repatriation basis of Public Sector Enterprises (PSEs) disinvested by Central Government subject to 1 percent of the paid up capital of the PSE concerned.

With effect from May 24, 1995 the permission was given to Euro issuing companies to retain the Euro issue proceeds as foreign currency deposits with the Bank's and Public Financial Institutions in India, which could be converted into Indian rupee only as and when expenditure for the approved end uses were incurred. With effect from November 25, 1995 companies were permitted to remit funds into India in anticipation of the use of funds for approved end uses. Moreover the existing ceiling for the use of issue proceeds for general corporate restructuring including working capital requirements were raised from 15 percent to 25 percent of the GDR issues.

During 1996-97, FIIs were allowed to invest up to 100 percent of their funds in debt instruments of Indian companies effective January 15, 1997. With effect from March 8, 1997, FIIs were allowed to invest in Government of India dated securities up to 30 percent, under the automatic route, the ceiling for lump sum payment of technical know-how fee had been increased from ₹ 1 crore to US$ 2 million with effect from November 5, 1996. With effect from January 17, 1997, the government allowed under the Automatic Approval route inclusion in Annexure-III of the Statement of Industrial Policy 1991 the following:

1. 3 categories of industries/items elating to mining activities for foreign equity up to 50 percent.
2. 13 additional categories of industries/items for foreign equity up to 51 percent.
3. 9 categories of industries/items for foreign equity up to 74 percent.

During 1997-98, foreign direct investment was allowed in sixteen non-banking financial services through the Foreign Investment Promotion Board. Expanding the scope of "automatic route" for foreign direct investments, the Government of India approved 13 additional categories of Industries/ items under services sector for foreign equity participation up to 51 percent of the equity. There were 3 items relating to mining activity up to 50 percent foreign equity participation and 9 categories of industries/activities up to 74 percent foreign equity participation.

As a part of the liberalized policy, the RBI decided to permit foreign banks operating in India to remit their profits or surplus to their head offices without the approval of the Reserve Bank. The Reserve Bank also allowed branches of foreign companies operating in India to remit profits to their head offices without the prior approval of the Reserve Bank. Also the Authorized Dealers (ADs) were permitted to provide forward cover to FIIs in respect of their fresh investment in equity in India as well as to cover the appreciation in the marked value of their existing investments in India w.e.f. June 12, 1998. The ADs were given the option of extending the cover fund-wise or FII-wise according to their operational feasibility. The same facility was extended to NRIs/OCBs for their portfolio investments w.e.f. June 16, 1998.

As per the 1997-98 guidelines the individual and aggregate portfolio investment ceiling for NRIs/OCBs/PIOs could be exclusive of the individual portfolio investment ceiling of 10 percent and aggregate portfolio investment ceiling of 30 percent of the paid up capital for FIIs. The aggregate investment ceiling for NRIs/OCBs/PIOs could be 10 percent of the paid up capital of companies listed on stock exchanges. The ceiling could be raised to 24 percent of the paid up capital by passing a General Body Resolution to that effect. The investment limit by a single NRI/OCB/PIO in the shares of a company under the portfolio investment scheme could continue to he 5 percent of the paid up capital. As per the Reserve Bank of India guidelines, Indian companies did not require the Bank's permission for the purpose of receiving inward remittance and issue of shares to NRI/OCB investors under the 100 percent scheme.

In August 1999, a Foreign Investment Implementation Authority (FIIA) was established within the Ministry of Industry in order to ensure that approvals for foreign investments (including NRI investments) were quickly translated into actual investment inflows and that proposals fructify into projects. In particular, in cases where FIPB clearance was needed, approval time was reduced to 30 days.

With a view to expand the FIIs category, the government permitted foreign corporate and high net worth individuals to invest through SEBI registered FIIs.

Such investments were subjected to a sub-limit for FII portfolio investments of 24 percent in a single company. The government also permitted SEBI registered domestic fund managers to manage foreign funds for investment in the Indian capital market through the portfolio investment route provided the funds were channelled through internationally recognized financial institutions and subject to the reporting requirements as applicable to FIIs.

In March 1999, the RBI issued a notification granting general permission to Mutual Funds for issuing units to NRIs/PIOs/OCBs subject to certain specified norms, thereby dispensing with the existing procedure of obtaining prior permission. In addition, the RBI simplified the approval in respect of NRIs/PIOs/OCBs by granting them general permission in lieu of a case by case approval procedure in a large number of areas. This included acceptance of deposits by Indian companies, investment in air taxi operations, sale of shares in stock exchanges, transfer of shares/bonds/debentures and immovable property to charitable trusts/organizations in India as gift, raising of loans by resident individuals/proprietorship concerns on non-repatriable basis, issue of commercial papers by Indian companies to NRIs etc.

Foreign owned Indian holding companies were hitherto required to obtain prior approval of the FIPB for downstream investment. They had been permitted to make such investments within permissible equity limits through the automatic route provided such holding companies bring in the requisite funds from abroad. Also, the need to obtain prior approval of the FIPB for increasing foreign equity within already approved limits had been dispensed with in all cases where the original project cost was up to ₹ 600 crore.

Considering the enhanced opportunities of Indian software companies for expanding globally, operational norms governing their overseas investments and mode of financing acquisition of overseas software companies had been liberalized. In December 1999, a notification was issued by the Ministry of Finance permitting Indian software companies, which are listed in foreign exchanges and have already floated ADR/GDR issues, to acquire foreign software companies and issue ADRs/GDRs without reference to the Government of India or the Reserve Bank of India up to the value limit of US$ 100 million. For acquisitions beyond US$ 100 million, proposals would require examination by a Special Composite Committee in the RBI.

Current Policy for Foreign Investment

The sweeping changes introduced since 1991 mark a radical departure from the past and reflect a positive approach towards foreign capital. The changes provide freedom to foreign investors to enter into Indian industry. Under the ongoing policy phase the thrust is on providing access to capital, technology and market in order to induce greater industrial efficiency and integration of the domestic economy with the global economy. FDI is permitted in almost all manufacturing industries (except six specified industries of strategic concern reserved for the state, i.e. plantations, housing and real estate. domestic trading print media, defence and strategic industries). The enlarged spheres for FDI entry now include mining, oil exploration refining and marketing, power generation and telecommunication, which were earlier reserved for the state sector. Under the new policy, foreign direct investments are also permitted in tourist and hotel industries and trading companies engaged in exports in the service sector. Clearly the sectors opened to FDI now are much larger as compared to the earlier policy.

If we compare the openness in Indian policy in terms of the sphere of operation with the policies of major competing countries we find that in China FDI is encouraged in most manufacturing and agricultural activities. Another country that has opened agriculture to FDI is Thailand. Generally, however, FDI is not permitted in agriculture and mining is most other competing Asian countries. Generally, manufacturing industries open to FDI in all the countries. In case of service industries there are wide variations. In China, all service industries (except hotels) are closed to foreign investment. On the other hand, in Thailand, FDI is permitted in almost all service industries. India, like most other Asian countries, stays in between the two extreme policy stances.

The most striking feature of the present liberalization policy in India is the freedom provided to the level of foreign equity participation. In the earlier policy phases, the attitude was quite rigid with respect to foreign equity ownership and control. It was insisted that FDI should be accompanied by technology transfer agreements. And, foreign ownership exceeding 40 percent of equity was granted only in exceptional cases. In striking contrast, under the liberalization policy, it is not necessary that FDI is accompanied by foreign technology agreements.

And FDI is given automatic approval up to 51 percent foreign equity in the listed priority industries, which cover most, manufacturing activities including software development and those related to hotel and tourism. Besides, there is no upper bound for foreign equity, even 100 percent foreign equity is permitted with prior approval permission is given freely to 100 percent foreign equity in the power sector and wholly export-oriented industries, all manufacturing activities in special economic zones in the telecommunication sector for internet service providers, infrastructure providers and electronic mail and voice mail. Further, the government presently has a liberal approach towards non-resident Indians (NRIs) investment.

NRIs and overseas corporate bodies (OCBs) can invest up to 100 percent in real estate sector and in certain other high priority industries. Clearly, the change in the government's attitude is basic in the sense that FDI is also looked upon as a channel of financial resources for investment independent of foreign technology transfer and foreign majority equity (and hence foreign control) is freely allowed to attract FDI inflows into priority industries.

To put the Indian policy in a comparative perspective it can be seen that in China, foreign majority is decided on case-by-case basis with 100 percent foreign ownership permitted in export-oriented and high technology industries. In Malaysia, foreign ownership is permitted in exports-oriented and high technology industries, though the guidelines in this regard are flexible. In Indonesia, a minimum 20 percent local participation is insisted upon in all foreign investments with local equity holding being increased to 51 percent within 20 years. In Thailand, foreign majority participation is prohibited in category 'A' industries (for example, rice farming, professional services) and restricted in category 'B' (for example, pharmaceutical products, trade, hotel, etc.). Foreign direct investment (including foreign majority equity) can enter even without permit in category 'C' industries, which include nearly all-manufacturing activities. In South Korea, there is no restriction on foreign participation in equity capital with prior approval. Generally, a large number of Asian countries permit foreign majority ownership in manufacturing but limit foreign ownership to minority in service industries.

Thus, Indian policy compares perhaps better than those of her major competitors do like China and Malaysia to the extent that in a large number of manufacturing industries (including some service industries), foreign majority ownership is freely allowed without any restriction. It is instructive that India's automatic approval of equity up to 51 percent is a unique process, which goes a long way in making Indian policy on FDI transparent. This leads us to the examination of the transparency in approval procedure.

Most countries have an approval requirement for the entry of foreign direct investment. In India, one of the irritants in the earlier policy phases has been the cumbersome procedure involved in the implementation of the regulatory policy. Apart from the delays, the bureaucratic discretion has been in built into the procedure of granting approval on a case-by-case basis. As compared to the earlier policy phase a distinctive feature of the liberalization. Policy phase is the simplification of procedures.

South Korea is the only other country, where automatic approval system exists, though it is confined to minority interest under certain conditions. South Korea has a well-defined regulation governing foreign investment and its "negative list system" with prohibited and restricted sectors, reflects the stability and transparency so important to an attractive FDI policy.

In India, all cases other than those coming under the parameters of automatic approval require prior scrutiny, and clearance of the Government. Foreign Investment Promotion Board (FIPB) or the Secretariat (SIA) clears such proposals for industrial approval. It must be appreciated that the approval requirement in China is higher and more rigid than in India.

Indian policy on transfer of technology has also been made liberal since 1991. Like FDI, there is the provision for automatic approval for technology agreements related to high priority industries within specified parameters. Similar facilities are available for other industries as well if such agreements do not require the expenditure of foreign exchange. Other liberalization measures include the freedom to use foreign trade names in the domestic market, which was not allowed earlier. The hiring of foreign technicians and foreign testing of indigenously developed technologies does not require prior clearance as prescribed earlier.

In short, as against the earlier practice of getting government's prior approval involving delays and uncertainty, the firms are at present free to negotiate terms of technology transfer with their foreign counterparts according to their own commercial judgements. Besides, there exists liberal external commercial borrowings and debt servicing norms. No ceiling has been placed on raising Global Depository Receipts (GDRs)/American Depository Receipts (ADRs)/Foreign Currency Convertible Bonds (FCCBs). Overseas business acquisitions have also been permitted through the ADR/GDR route. Indian companies in IT sector have been permitted to issue ADR/GDR linked stock options to permanent employees of its subsidiary companies incorporated in India or abroad. Allowing foreign institutional investors (FIIs) to invest up to 49 percent of the capital of the companies is a welcome change for Indian companies.

In a nutshell, the sweeping changes introduced since 1991 mark a radical departure from the past and reflect a positive approach towards foreign collaboration. The changes provide freedom to foreign investors to enter into Indian industry. In terms of openness to FDI entry, the prevailing Indian policy is not unfavourably placed in terms of competitiveness with other major FDI-receiving countries in Asia.

Foreign Investment and Domestic Resources

An examination of the direct contribution of foreign companies to host countries' total investment requires that the investment of these companies be compared with the investment of domestic firms. But countries typically do not disaggregate their investment expenditures accordingly: FDI inflows are, therefore, used as a proxy, for measuring investment by foreign firms. Based on this measure and gross fixed capital formation (GFCF) as a measure of total Investment in host countries, the following trends emerge:

1. During the past three decades, the importance of FDI relative to total investment has consistently increased in all country groups developed, developing and countries in Central and Eastern Europe. In the 1990s, this importance has become for the first time higher in developing countries than in developed countries, with the ratios of FDI inflows to GFCF for the developing countries amounting to 8.0 percent and 10.6 percent and for the developed countries the ratio amounting to 5.4 percent and 8.6 percent respectively, during 1985-90 and 1995-99.

2. In spite of its rapidly growing importance, FDI still plays, on average, a modest role in domestic investment in all country groups, indicating the potential for further growth in importance. In most countries, the ratio does not exceed 10 percent.

However, FDI flows underestimate total investment of foreign companies in host countries. The difference between the two measures (foreign companies' investment expenditure and FDI) can be attributed to two factors. One is that foreign companies can finance their investment expenditures from sources other than FDI inflows. The second factor is that FDI inflows include components that are not used for the financing of their investment expenditure.

Investment expenditure can he financed from sources external to the TNC system. These sources are the capital markets of the host countries and international financial markets. The share of funds raised in both host country markets and international capital markets in total financing of foreign companies is quite significant. This explains a large part of the difference between total investment expenditures of foreign companies and FDI inflows. This difference should not be large in host developing countries, because borrowing costs in these countries tend to be higher than costs in developed countries and in international financial markets. But the high cost of borrowing and underdeveloped financial markets in many developing countries do not discourage TNCs from local financing. Exchange rate and country risk considerations play a great role in financing decisions.

As regards the second factor explaining the difference between investment of foreign affiliates and FDI inflows generated by them, the latter may include flows for mergers and acquisitions, which do not contribute to a host country's capital formation at the moment of entry.

Another non-investment component is intra-country loans. Although mergers and acquisitions is not investment in new productive assets at the moment of entry, they may lead to investment in the future through sequential investment. It cannot be ruled out that loans are used to finance investment in fixed capital.

The importance of these components for FDI flows varies. As regards loans, the data available for selected countries show that they accounted for 18 percent of total FDI inflows in these countries in 1990-98. There was no difference between developed and developing countries in this regard. There was also no clear trend. Rather, the share of loans in total inflows fluctuated from year to year, within a range of eight percent to 38 percent in developer countries and three percent to 25 percent in developing countries.

As regards mergers and acquisitions, they appear to be a

dominant component of FDI inflows in developed countries, while, green field projects were the dominant mode of entry of TNCs into developing countries. Recently, there is a trend towards an increase of mergers and acquisitions in some developing countries. Many of these deals relate to privatization and therefore are likely to lead to sequential investment. Although mergers and acquisitions do not have a direct impact on a host country's investment at the moment of entry, they may have an indirect impact on this investment.

Foreign Capital and Technology/Knowledge Transfer

The discussion of FDI and technology needs a sound understanding of how firms in developing countries actually become proficient in using technology. Importing 'and mastering technologies in developing countries is not as easy as earlier assumed. Technology is not sold like physical products, in fully embodied forms. It has important tacit elements that need effort to master. It often faces an uncertain environment where the skills, information, networks and credit needed are not readily available. Enterprises have to interact intensively with other agents. All these features mean that technology development faces extensive coordination problems, externalities, missing markets and cumulative effects.

More importantly, firms may face learning problems. The diffusion of technologies even in industrial countries poses challenges. In developing countries, it is generally far more difficult. Mastering new technology is not just a once-for-all task. It is a process that requires continuous upgrading and deepening of all kinds of intellectual capital, as well as of supporting networks and institutions. Without this, countries can remain at the bottom of the technology ladder where their competitive edge lies in simple assembly or processing based on cheap labour. Once wages rise they lose this edge. Thus, as they master the simpler elements of technology, they have to move into more advanced technological capabilities. As technologies change, they have to upgrade their own capabilities to remain competitive. As they gain competence in simple activities, they have to move into more advanced ones. Thus, at each stage, learning needs new knowledge, skills and organization.

There can he the risks of market and institutional failure and they can be particularly high where learning, information, coordination and externalities are involved. The ability of governments to overcome them, create new markets and strengthen institutions is then the crucial factor in technology development.

1. **Technology Generation:** While international innovative activity by TNCs is of long standing, differences are emerging in the new context. There is now a greater spread of firms conducting R&D outside their home countries. Adaptation and technical support are still the main motives for affiliate R&D, but there is an increasing trend towards tapping into foreign centres of innovative excellence. The changing strategies of TNCs are leading to more "asset seeking" overseas investment.

2. **Technology Transfer:** Foreign enterprises transfer technologies in two ways: internalized to affiliates under their ownership and control, and externalized to other firms. Internalized transfer takes the form of direct investment and is, by definition, the preserve of TNCs. It is difficult to measure and compare directly the amounts of technology transferred in this manner. Measured by payments for royalties and license fees, a substantial part of the payments is made intra-firm. As rising costs may force firms into more technology-based alliances, internalization can also be seen to encompass technology transfers among clusters of innovative TNCs. Policy liberalization by host governments also tends to favour internalization strategies.

Externalized modes of transfer by TNCs take a variety of forms: minority joint ventures, franchising, capital goods sales, licenses, technical assistance, subcontracting or original equipment-manufacturing arrangements. TNCs are not the only source of externalized technology, of course. But they are very important in high-technology activities and in providing entire "packages', i.e. technology together with management, marketing, etc.

Foreign Capital and Exports

The impact study of the influence of foreign collaboration and in particular, foreign direct investment, on the export performance of the Indian industry assumes significance as the ongoing liberalization policy is based on the belief that FDI helps resolving foreign exchange constraints to development by its contribution to increased exports apart from bringing in net resource inflows on the capital account of the balance of payments. To quote from the Government's Industrial Policy Statement of 1991, "Foreign investment would bring attendant advantages of technology transfer, marketing expertise, introduction of modern managerial techniques and new possibilities for promotion of exports". The rationale of FDI liberalization policy for a developing country rests on the idea of the relatively better export performance of TNCs.

This is derived from the neo-factor endowment and neo-technology theories of international trade. In this theoretical framework, subsidiaries of foreign companies are generally considered to be better placed to tap international markets than their local counterparts in view of their captive access to the information and marketing networks of their parent enterprises. Besides, they have easy access to parent firms' advanced technology and also to monopoly advantages of patent, trade mark and other investment-related intellectual property of parent firms, which facilitate their efforts to enhance exports from the host-country. However, the theoretical case needs careful empirical investigation for each particular host-country. Therefore, any empirical inquiry into the export performance of Indian subsidiaries of foreign companies only, as a group in the Indian industry, will be rewarding intellectually.

So far as the literature on the subject with reference to India is concerned, few studies are quoted here: Lall has found that foreign presence and the extent of foreign share holding are positively associated with export propensities, whereas many others such as Subramanian and Pillai, Kumar and Pandey have not found empirical evidence supporting the theory of better export performance of foreign enterprises. All the studies, however, relate to the pre-liberalization period. It is possible that the market distortion effect of the protective policy regime would have made domestic market more profitable than exporting, and made the foreign firms to orient their strategies biased against exporting from India, despite their inherent advantages and the governments' incentives for export promotion.

To the extent that the situation has changed with the introduction of outward-oriented liberalization policy, it stands to reason that the behaviour of the subsidiaries of foreign companies would reflect signs of significantly better export performance. This proposition stands valid also in the case of the existing firms established earlier during the protective policy regime, as they are now free to modernize, diversify, expand and to perform better in their export activities.

Analysis of Operational Environment

India's economic reforms and trade liberalization policies contributed to a dramatic increase in its economic growth in the mid-1990s. Larger flows of inward foreign investment and increased international trade helped India achieve annual average growth rates of 7 percent from 1993 to 1996. Economic growth slowed, however, in 1997 and, according to a new WTO Secretariat report on India's trade policies and practices, India should continue liberalizing its trade and investment regime to ensure strong and stable economic growth.

The WTO Secretariat report and a policy statement prepared by the Government of India, provides the basis for a review of India's trade policies and practices. The focus of the WTO's report is on India's policy and trade measures affecting imports, exports and production. The report notes that India recognizes the need to continue economic reforms, with an increased emphasis on improving its industrial infrastructure. The latter has proved to be a constraint on expanding economic activity and stimulating exports. Other measures under consideration are reductions in tariffs and non-tariff measures, reforming the subsidies structure (estimated to account for 14 percent of GDP), and restructuring public sector enterprises.

The Indian Government initiated a major programme of economic reform and liberalization in 1991. Reforms in the manufacturing sector have been widespread, including reductions in average tariff rates, import licensing restrictions for industrial inputs and capital goods and compulsory industrial licensing; the agricultural sector and consumer goods trade have, as yet, been relatively untouched by government reform efforts. While there has been some liberalization, there has been no change in the structure of agricultural incentives and subsidies.

India's financial services are gradually being liberalized while significant headway has already been made in liberalizing telecommunications. Other services, such as shipping, roads, ports and air, are beginning to open up, but, the report states, foreign participation remains relatively low and significant administrative barriers remain. India amended its Copyright Law in 1994 to comply with its obligations under the Trade-Related Intellectual Property Rights (TRIPS) Agreement. As a developing country, India has until the year 2000 for most products, but until 2005 for some goods, to comply with the TRIPS Agreement but is currently required to provide means for receiving product patent application in certain areas. On this issue, a decision by a WTO dispute settlement panel and the Appellate Body has stated that India was in violation of its obligation.

Tariffs have been reduced from an average of 71 percent in 1993 to an average of 35 percent. The report notes, however, that the tariff structure remains complex and that escalation remains high in several industries, notably paper and paper products, printing and publishing, wood and wood products, and food, beverages and tobacco. In general, bound tariffs remain substantially higher than applied rates, especially on agricultural products.

Conclusion

It is seen that the policy framework in India dealing with foreign private investment has changed from cautious welcome policy during 1948-66 to selective and restrictive policy during 1967 to 1979. In the decade of eighties, it was the policy having partial liberalization with many regulations. Liberal investment climate has been created only since 1991. The period from 1991 till date the characterized by transparency and openness and is intended to seek more foreign investment inflows.

Recently, the Government of India cleared the most-awaited reform measure, allowing foreign direct investment (FDI) in multi-brand retail up to 51 percent, paving the way for international multi-brand retailers to set up business in India. This apart liberalized FDI norms for aviation, broadcasting, insurance and pension sectors have also been cleared.

However, there are some specific aspects, (e.g. lack of transparency in the approval of FIPs/SIA cases, regulations at the levels of state governments for accessing operating facilities and rates of taxes and tariffs especially with regard to corporate taxation, capital gains tax and customs duty) which need detailed review and revisions for rendering the Indian environment relatively more competitive for FDI inflows than before. A cross-sectional comparison of the various aspects of the current Indian policy regime on foreign capital indicates that in terms of the openness of the policy environment, India does not rank much below the other foreign capital seeking countries in Asia.

End Note

1. Government of India, Planning Commission, *First Five Year Plan* (1951-56), pp. 437-438.

References

Anil Das Gupta and Bibek Debroy, "Salavaging the WTO's Future: Doha and Beyond", Rajiv Gandhi Institute for Contemporary Studies, New Delhi (2001).

C.M. Correa, "New International Standards for Intellectual Property: Impact on Technology Flows and Innovation in Developing Countries", Science and Public Policies (1997).

D.S. Swainy, "Multinational Corporations in World Economy", Alps International Publishers, Delhi (1980).

Denise E. Konan, "The Need for Common Investment Measures With ASEAN", ASEAN Economic Bulletin, Vol. 12, No. 3, (March 1996).

Dillon, K. Burke and Others, "Recent Developments in External, Debt Restructuring", IMF Occasional Paper No. 40, Washington, (October 1985).

Economic and Social Commission for Asia and the Pacific, "The Future WTO Agenda and Developing Countries", UNCTAD, United Nations, New York (2000).

Navaretti, Giorgio B. and Anthony J. Venables (2004), "Multinational Firms in the World Economy", Princeton and Oxford: Princeton University Press.

Pradhan, J.P. and M.K. Sahoo (2005), "Outward Foreign Direct Enterprises", Consultancy report prepared for the UNCTED'S Global Players Project.

R. Vernonon, "Review Transnational Corporations, Market Structure and Competitive Policy", Economic Development and Cultural Change, (January 1999).

Razin, Assaf, Yona Rubinstein, and Efram Sadka (2004), "Fixed Costs and FDI: The Conflicting Effects of Productivity Shocks," NBER Working Paper No. 10864.

Stanley Fisher, "Capital Account Liberalization and the Role of the IMF", Washington, IMF, (September 1997).

Swenson, Deborah L. (1994), "The Impact of US Tax Reform on Foreign Direct Investment in the United States," *Journal of Public Economics,* 54(2): 243-66.

Swenson, Deborah L. (2004), "Foreign Investment and Mediation of Trade Flows".

T.A. Stewart, "Intellectual Capital", London (1997).

Tomlin, KaSaundra M. (2000), "The Effects of Model Specification on Foreign Direct Investment Models: An Application of Count Data Models," *Southern Economic Journal,*

US Census (2001), "US Goods Trade: Imports and Exports by Related Parties-2000", U.S. Department of Commerce News, available at:
www.census.gov/foreign-trade/Press-Release/2000pr/aip/related-party.html.

UNCTAD (2006), "World Investment Report 2006-FDI from Developing and Transition Economics: Implications for Development", United Nations.

Wei, Shang-Jin (2000a), "How Taxing is Corruption on International Investors?", *Review of Economics and Statistics.*

Wei, Shang-Jin (2000b), "Local Corruption and Global Capital Flows", *Brookings Papers on Economic Activity.*

Wheeler, David, and Ashoka Mody (1992), "International Investment Location Decisions: The Case of U.S. Firms," *Journal of International Economics*, 33(1-2).

Yeaple, Stephen R. (2003a), "The Complex Integration Strategies of Multinationals and Cross Country Dependencies in the Structure of Foreign Direct Investment," *Journal of International Economics.*

Yeaple, Stephen R. (2003b), "The Role of Skill Endowments in the Structure of US Outward Foreign Direct Investment," *Review of Economics and Statistics.*

Zhan, "Trannationalization and Outward Investment: The Case of Chinese Firms, Transnational Corporations", (April 1995).

2

FDI in Print Media

D. Boopath

India has one of the most transparent and liberal FDI regimes among the emerging and developing economies. By FDI regime we mean those restrictions that apply to foreign nationals and entities but not to Indian nationals and Indian owned entities. The differential treatment is limited to a few entry rules, spelling out the proportion of equity that the foreign entrant can hold in an Indian (registered) company or business. There are a few banned sectors and some sectors with limits on foreign equity proportion. The entry rules are clear and well defined and equity limits for foreign investment in selected sectors such as *telecom* quite explicit and well known.

Some factors are more relevant for first time investors with no previous experience of investment in India. Though economic reforms welcoming foreign capital were introduced in the nineties it does not seem so far to be really evident in our overall attitude.

There is a lingering perception abroad that foreign investors are still looked at with some suspicion. There is also a view that some unhappy episodes in the past have a multiplier effect by adversely affecting the business environment in India. Besides the "made in India" label is not conceived by the world as synonymous with quality (Planning Commission, 2002).

Growth of the Press: 1950s to Satellite TV

The growth of the press, particularly the Indian language segment of it, exposed an increasingly large number of people who could access it thanks to spreading *literacy,* to political debates and discussions and contributed to a heightening of their political consciousness. This in turn not only generated further interest in reading newspapers and increased demand for them but also evoked greater interest in news and comment first on radio and then on television. This, however, would not have led to a massive increase in newspaper readership and television viewership but for the emergence of a large middle class with disposable incomes (Karlekar, H., 1998).

The size of their class has never been precisely computed. A report in the *Indian Express* in January 1996 which puts it at 250 million, seems, however, to be in tune with the generally-held estimate (Ghosh, B., 1996). The increase in the literacy rate from 18.33 percent of the population in 1951 to 52.11 percent in 1991 and 74.04 in 2011 (Census, 2011), resulting in a widely expanded readership, also accounts for increased circulation of newspapers and periodicals.

In India, the influence of the consumer culture is paramount over the middle classes and a section of the working class. Societal and cultural changes being generally evolutionary, it is difficult to say exactly when it established its ascendency over a large section of the country's population.

Since, as a category, they generally have a much higher purchasing power than those who can read or write only an Indian language, the proportion of those who can afford to buy one or more newspapers or journals is much higher among them (Padmaja, 2008). In many cases, the leaders who came to power in the newly-formed states after Independence helped Indian language papers to grow by extending to them requisite facilities.

Large parts of the Indian media community, not surprisingly, viewed Independence as a triumph. More importantly, the corporate, class, and ideological interests of newspaper proprietors closely coincided with those of the Indian state.

Perhaps predictably, the media developed, for the most

part, a less-than adversarial relationship with the new political dispensation in New Delhi. Although India's first Prime Minister, Jawaharlal Nehru, was not without his critics in the media, newspapers for the most part treated government with a respect bordering on deference.

Yet by the mid-1970s, growing strains in India's political life-and widespread disenchantment with the Congress Party's regime-begun to reflect itself in media reportage. In June 1975, Prime Minister Indira Gandhi declared a state of emergency and imposed full-scale press censorship. Although the country had experienced emergency regulations during the wars of 1962 and 1971, censorship had not been imposed on either occasion (Swami, P., 2009).

The transformation of the Indian newspaper and magazine industry into a business began post-1977, after the emergency was lifted. The Janata government, which came to power in the post-Emergency elections, repealed most of the regressive laws.

In three years—between the depths of the 'emergency' in 1976 and 1979, the year before Indira Gandhi returned to power as prime ministe—newspaper circulation rose 40 percent for dailies and 34 percent for periodicals. The country was sharply and bitterly divided between the supporters and opponents of Indira Gandhi; political debates were acrimonious and exchanges accusatory. The print media too reflected the cleavage and reports, political analyses and editorials were often trenchant (Jeffrey, R., 2000).

After the 'emergency', central and state governments continued to experiment with ways to control the press, but the panacea of creating "small" newspapers and breaking the nexus between "big business" and newspapers went out of fashion. In part, this reflected the growing assertion of Indian capitalism in the 1980s. From around the middle of the 1980s, when the consumer culture began to spread in the country, even the print media started becoming increasingly entertainment-oriented and trivialized in its content and preoccupations. But it also resulted from an understanding that big newspapers could be politicians' friends. Political rhetoric adapted: a capitalist press was not necessarily an evil press (Nayar, K., 2007).

For Indian-language newspapers this acceptance was important because it helped to encourage investment and reinforce efforts to attract major advertisers. As politicians courted successful newspapers in their regions, the newspaper business looked safer and more secure (Nobrega, W. and A. Sinha, 2008).

For the Indian media, emergency rule proved to be a transformative experience. In the decades after, a new generation of journalists worked to erase the shame of that period by mobilizing in defence of press freedoms. An increasingly feisty and sometimes irreverent journalism was born, characterized by an adversarial relationship with authority (Swami, P., 2009; Jeffrey, R., 2010). This new journalism coincided with a revolution in media reach and influence.

FDI in Print Media: First Phase

Following the recommendations of the First Press Commission, the central government (Jawaharlal Nehru cabinet) had, in 1955, decided that no foreign-owned newspaper or periodical should, in future, be published in India and that foreign newspapers and periodicals, which dealt mainly with news and current affairs should not be allowed to bring out their editions in India. Another decision taken by the government in 1956 was that communication facilities should be granted to foreign news agencies only where distribution of news within the country would be effected through an Indian news agency owned and managed by Indians, and which would have full and final authority in the selection of foreign news and their distribution and which would also be in a position to supply Indian news to the foreign news agencies (Sarkaria, R.S., 1996).

Technically, nothing stopped a foreign magazine from selling in India or launching an Indian edition or investing in a publishing company in India. However, the 1955 cabinet resolution, which never became a law or an ordinance, remained the defining word on this issue for decades.

The different governments at the centre have considered the resolution off and on and have come to endorse the resolution. The Editors Guild of India and the Indian Newspapers Society (INS) have also rejected entry of foreigners in the print media more than once (Nayar, K., 2000).

New Economic Policy (NEP) and Print Media

1991 was truly a turning point for the Indian economy. The congress party returned to power amidst the assassination of Rajiv Gandhi. The Congress government under P.V. Narashima Rao decided to break away from the past, charting out a new market-oriented growth path. The real architect of this new model happened to be the present Prime Minister Manmohan Singh, who then headed the finance portfolio.

Creeping economic liberalization had begun in the 1980s, but it gained momentum only in the 1980s. India ran out of foreign exchange in 1991, and was forced to mortgage its gold reserves. When the process of economic reforms began in 1991, one of the prescribed structural changes was the deregulation of investment to provide space for the private sector and thereby permit forces of competitive efficiency to emerge. The Soviet Union's collapse in 1991 showed that the answer did not lie in more socialism. There was no equivalent of Ronald Reagan or Margaret Thatcher in India. Liberalization was seen as a pragmatic way to meet the compulsions of an empty treasury. This led to half-backed liberalization, with reforms that were gradual, partial and often inconsistent.

All opposition parties predicted that economic reforms would be a disaster, and said that, like Africa and Latin America, structural adjustment would mean a lost decade of development. Left intellectuals predicted that multinationals would decimate Indian companies. In fact, the reform succeeded faster than even *The Economic Times* predicted. Hence liberal policies were continued by the Left-dominated United Front government of 1996-98.The NDA (National Democratic Alliance) government headed by Atal Bihari Vajpayee (BJP) that came to power in 1998 continued and deepened the reform process. Yashwant Sinha (former finance minister) in 1998-2002 turned out to be a committed liberaliser, despite making some initial swadeshi noises (Kohli-Khandekar, V., 2010).

The most visible impact of liberalisation was experienced in sectors like aviation, banking and finance, media and entertainment and of course telecom.

It is evident that as India enters the new millennium, the ball game for India's news media—the press, television and radio—is dramatically different from what it was sixty years ago. It can also be seen that the two established media traditions, associated with the press and the broadcast media respectively, are no longer quite what they were widely recognized to be for most of the twentieth century.

Jeffrey (2010) traces the growth of the Indian language press from 1977-1999. He puts it down to five factors: improved technology, steadily expanding literacy, better purchasing power, aggressive publishing and political excitement. Jeffrey's work is by far the most comprehensive and insightful piece of writing on the Indian press. With the impressive spurt in the growth rates of newspapers (in terms of circulation as well as advertising volume and revenue) in the 1990's, a trend arrested by semi-recessionary conditions in Indian industry and advertising during 1997-1999, the press appears to be a bigger player than ever on the Indian social and political scene, even if it still reaches less than half the adult Indian population (Ram, N., 2000).

Interestingly, the Indian response to the challenges and opportunities presented by globalization has varied sharply across the principal media sectors. For the press sector, it seems more than fortuitous that 'media globalization hit India at a time of extraordinary growth' in the language press, with the changing structure of national politics giving regional parties a new salience and role and boosting Indian language newspaper circulations (Thussu, 1998).

Should foreign players, individuals or corporate organizations, be allowed to publish newspapers in India or enter into joint ventures or collaborations with Indian parties for the same purpose? This question was vigorously debated for a while in the first half of the 1990s. Powerful foreign media interests, led by Murdoch's News Corporation, in alliance with certain Indian press proprietors and the Indian finance ministry, lobbied for allowing foreign players in (Ninan, S., 2008).

At one point, it looked as if the pro-changers would carry the day. When a five-member ministerial group set up by the P.V. Narasimha Rao government submitted the outcome of its study of the issue, the majority opinion in the group favoured allowing foreign players in. After a murky and confused phase, political opposition and broad-based opposition within the press sector built up powerfully and the government was forced to abandon its inclination to reverse longstanding national policy barring foreign ownership within the press sector (Ram, N., 1994).

FDI in Print Media: Second Phase

A tremendous degree of interest was generated during 2001-2002, for instance, over the long-standing question of permitting foreign direct investment (FDI) in the print media, which was addressed and deliberated upon by lawmakers and the Ministry of Information and Broadcasting. A parliamentary standing committee on information technology submitted a report under the direction of Sushma Swaraj, the then Minister for Information and Broadcasting (India Book of the Year, 2002).

On this occasion it was between newspaper establishments rather than between them and the government. Finally, under pressure from many publishers, the government (the then ruling Bhartiya Janata Party-BJP) allowed 26 percent FDI into Indian print in June 2002. This was amended in 2005 to allow foreign institutional investors (FIIs) and further amendments were made in March 2006 (Jeffrey, R., 2010).

Since 2002, the government has cleared 17 proposals for foreign direct investment (FDI) in print media. In all, 183 Indian editions of specialty magazines have been allowed (Saraf, A., 2008). This is besides the 116 cases where foreign investment has been allowed for specialty magazines.

In many ways 2002 was a watershed year for the print media amid changing look and increasing readership in the regional languages. Issues of credibility, control, and content emerged, with professional and commercial interests often pulling in different directions (India Book of the Year, 2003). The outcome remains uncertain.

T.N. Ninan, former editor, *The Economic Times* and chairman and editorial director of Business Standard Ltd. in his valuable scholarship on the Indian print media, encompassing the FDI and FII, highlights a buoyant and dynamic situation.

The first deal under FDI in newspapers materialized in September 2003. In fact, two deals were announced–one involving 13.8 percent equity (although allowed up to 26 percent) in *Business Standard* by *Financial Times* of London, and the other in the *Hindustan Times* to the extent of 20 percent stake by an Australian investor, Henderson Global. What started as cooperation with editorial syndication of reports between *Business Standard* and *Financial Times* has culminated in a joint venture. Such an (exclusive) arrangement exists already for some years now between *The Financial Express* and *The Wall Street Journal* and more recently in the case of *The Asian Age* and *The New York Times*.

Foreign entry into the news segment was supposed to

shake things up, but it has not happened. The *International Herald Tribune* sells a few thousand copies, at ₹ 30 a piece, and the *Wall Street Journal* may do no better. In Delhi, Living Media (publisher of *India Today)* teamed up with Britain's *Daily Mail* to launch *Mail Today* in late 2007, and would appear to face a long uphill task in a market dominated by the *Hindustan Times* and the *Times of India.*

The situation is slightly different when it comes to international magazines: they have come in because of low entry barriers and a smaller ticket size when it comes to investment. So we have *Car* and *Autocar, Vogue* and *Cosmopolitan, Scientific American* and *Harvard Business Review*–but niche titles only give the impression of proliferation. Essentially, they remain marginal players.

Foreign equity investments in existing titles have also made little difference: *Financial Times* invested in *Business Standard*, then pulled out. The Irish *Independent* has invested in *Jagran Prakashan,* but there is no action from the company in terms of new ventures, other than a foray into outdoor media (Ninan, T.N., 2009).

Recent Development

Earlier, in 2005, the government had relaxed its rules regarding local editions of foreign non-news magazines that saw a flood of foreign publishers like Conde Nast (publisher of fashion magazine *Vogue*), Rodale Inc. (publisher of women's health magazine *Prevention*), Axel Springer (publisher of auto magazine *Autobid*) and Time Inc. (publisher of *People*, a magazine that focuses on life of celebrities) rushing in to tie-up with Indian publishers.

For publishing in India, foreign publications would typically look for magazines that have some amount of financial strength, distribution network, brand equity and editorial contribution. At present, *Forbes* magazine has tied up with the media house TV 18 for its plans for India, while *Fortune* has been planning to bring out a country-specific edition, in alliance with the Ananda Bazaar Patrika (ABP) group of publications (Saraf, A., 2008).

From 2006 to 2008, the Indian print media attracted an investment of over ten billion rupees. The years 2007 and 2008 saw a record number of newspaper deals and launches.

The Union Cabinet in September 2008 cleared Information and Broadcasting Ministry's proposal on 'foreign news magazines' and their Indian editions. This proposal is in line with the existing foreign investment cap for newspapers (The Hindu, September 19, 2008).

Only Indian companies registered under the Indian Companies Act, 1956 henceforth be allowed to bring out Indian editions of foreign news magazines. A foreign newspaper provided at least, three-fourths of the directors on the Board of the resultant entity and all key executives and editorial staff have to be resident Indians. The new rule stipulates that the title of the magazine have to be registered by the Indian company with the Registrar of Newspapers for India (India Book of the Year, 2003; 2004).

While opening up this sector, the government has stipulated that only those magazines which are being published in the country of their origin might be allowed to enter India with an Indian edition. To ensure against fly-by-night operations, the policy also states that these periodicals should have been in print for at least five years running with a minimum circulation of 10,000 copies during the last fiscal in the country of origin (Saraf, A., 2008).

The new policy does not provide any parameters on the content of the Indian edition of foreign news magazines. The Indian edition can be either identical to the foreign magazine it ties up with or it can include locally generated material. The Indian publisher is also free to insert local advertisements (Ninan, S., 2008). The mast head of the foreign publication cannot be utilised and the credit has to be given as a prominent byline in the Indian publication. Before the policy was announced, U.K. based Dennis Publishing announced a joint venture with media Transasia, responsible for *Maxim* magazine in India to launch at least three new brands.

According to the industry estimates, the Indian magazine publishing market is expected to grow to ₹ 3,800 crore in 2012 from the current estimated size of ₹ 1,900 crore. Advertising is projected to grow at 16 percent (compared to circulation revenues of 10 percent) to reach ₹ 3,000 crore in 2012, from the current ₹ 1,400 crore.

In July, in a report titled Global Entertainment and Media Outlook 2008-12, Price Waterhouse Coopers (PwC), the world's largest professional services firm, has stated that India is one of the top three markets for global collaboration in entertainment and media because of a "relatively friendly foreign investment regime". The report also said that print publication advertising revenues in India generated US$ 2.5 billion in 2007. Sustained economic growth and entry of new breed of advertisers in India would ensure a steady print advertising compounded annual growth rate (CAGR) of about 15 percent annually (higher than the global projection of about 3 percent annually).

Conclusion

The Press Council of India in its official publications entitled, 'Future of Print Media-A Report' published in 2001 had come out with select observations. The Press Council of India (2001) has commented on 'synergic alliance' or equity participation in the shape of foreign direct investment (FDI). The Council opined that FDI should be allowed to break or halt the growing monopoly of a few media giants in India who offer uneven playground and unhealthy competition to small and medium papers. This opinion is based on the argument that if FDI can be allowed for even defence production there should not be any objection to allow it in the field of print media which needs funds for modernisation.

The foreign media is already there in the television and vigorous efforts are being made by it to enter the print media as well. It is eating into the grass roots of the Indian culture at incredible pace. Channels like FTV (Fashion Television) are nothing short of soft pornography. The foreign media which runs counter to our cultural values needs to be banned or at least regulated.

When a foreign investor considers making any new investment decision, it goes through four stages in the decision making process and action cycle, namely, *(a) screening, (b) planning, (c) implementing* and *(d) operating and expanding.* The biggest barrier for India is at the first, screening stage itself in the action cycle.

An attitudinal and mind set change towards FDI is necessary. This may be conceptually simple but practically difficult to change; changing foreign perception of India and making an attractive destination for FDI is a daunting challenge. The only method that is known to have worked in other countries is a clear and unambiguous message from the top leadership of the government conveying its importance to all organs of government. An alternative could be a well-designed publicity campaign bringing out the advantages that various countries have reaped from FDI.

References

Ghosh, B. (1996), *Consumer cult cashes in on credit cards*, Indian Express, Delhi, January 3, 1996.

Jeffrey, Robin (2000), *India's newspaper revolution; capitalism, politics and the Indian–language press, 1977-99*, Oxford University Press, New Delhi.

Jeffrey, Robin (2010), *India's newspaper revolution; capitalism, politics and the Indian–language press*, Oxford University Press, New Delhi.

Karlekar, Hiranmay (1998), *Media: mirror and the market*, in H. Karlekar (ed.), Independent India, The First Fifty Years, Oxford University Press, Delhi, pp. 504-534.

Kohli-Khandekar, Vanita (2010), *The Indian media business*, Response Books, New Delhi.

Nayar, Kuldip (2000), *The perils of opening the print media*, The Hindu, October 31, 2000.

Nayar, Kuldip (2007), *The perils of opening the print media*, in N. Lakshmaman (ed.), Writing a Nation: An Anthology of Indian Journalism, Rupa & Co., New Delhi, pp. 227-229.

Ninan, Sevanti (2008), *Changing fortunes*, The Hindu, October 26, 2008.

Ninan, T.N. (2009), *The Newspaper capital of the world*, in Business Standard, India 2009, Business Standard Limited, New Delhi, pp. 205-220.

Nobrega, W. and A. Sinha (2008), *Riding the Indian tiger, understanding India-the world's fastest growing market*, Wiley India Pvt. Ltd, New Delhi.

Padmaja, R (2008), *Marketing of Newspapers*, Kanishka Publishers and Distributors, New Delhi.

Planning Commission (2002), *Report of the Steering Group on Foreign Direct Investment*, Government of India, New Delhi.

Press Council of India (2001), *Future of print media: A report*, Press Council of India, New Delhi.

Ram, N. (2000), *The great Indian media bazaar: emerging trends and issues for the future*, in (ed.) Romila Thapar, India: Another Millennium, Penguin Books, New Delhi, pp. 241-292.

Ram, N. (1994), *Foreign media entry into the press-issues and implications*, Economic and Political Weekly, October (43).

Saraf, Anu (2008), *Turning a new page, Indian editions of foreign publications can now be published in India*, Business India, October, 20-November 2, (Issue No. 799), p. 124.

Sarkaria, R.S. (1996), *How good a watchdog is the press council*, in M.V. Desai and Sevanti Ninan (eds.), Beyond those Headlines: Insiders on the Indian Press, The Media Foundation, New Delhi, pp. 27-38.

Swami, P. (2009), *Breaking news: the media revolution*, in S. Gaugualy, L. diamond and M.F. Plattner (eds.), The State of India's Democracy, Oxford University Press, New Delhi, pp. 176-194.

Thursu, Daya Kishan (1998), *Localising the global: Zee TV in India'*, in Thussu (ed.), Electronic Empires: Global Media and Local Resistance, Arnold, London.

3

FDI Inflows into India in the Post-reforms Period

Rajesh C. Jampala, P. Adi Lakshmi and
Srinivasa Rao Dokku

Introduction

Foreign direct investment (FDI) is now recognized as an important driver of growth in the country. Government is, therefore, making all efforts to attract and facilitate FDI and investment from non-resident Indians (NRIs) including overseas corporate bodies (OCBs) that are predominantly owned by them, to complement and supplement domestic investment. To make the investment in India attractive, investment and returns on them are freely reparable, except where the approval is subject to specific conditions such as lock-in period on original investment, dividend cap, foreign exchange neutrality, etc. as per the notified sartorial policy. The condition of dividend balancing that was applicable to FDI in 22 specified consumer goods industries stands withdrawn for dividends declared after 14th July 2000.

A country with a developing economy cannot depend on it domestic savings along to fuel its economy's rapid growth. The domestic savings of India are 25 percent of its GDP. But this can provide only a 2 to 3 percent growth of its economy on annual basis. India has to maintain 8 to 10 percent growth for period of two decades to reach the levels of advanced nations and to wipe out widespread poverty of its people. The gap is to be covered by inflow of foreign investment along with advanced technology. India, among the European investors, is believed to be a good investment despite political uncertainty, bureaucratic hassles, shortage of power and infrastructural deficiencies. It presents a vast potential for overseas investment and is actively encouraging entry of foreign players into the market. In India, foreign direct investment (FDI) is permitted under following forms of investments:

1. Through financial collaborations.
2. Through joint ventures and technical collaborations
3. Through capital market.
4. Through private placements or preferential allotments.

Advantages of FDI in India

Foreign investment plays an important role in the long-term economic development of a country by: (a) augmenting availability of capital (b) enhancing competitiveness of the domestic economy through transfer of technology, (c) strengthening infrastructure, (d) raising productivity, (e) generating new employment opportunities and (f) boosting exports. Foreign investment, therefore, is a strategic instrument of development policy.

In the wake of economic liberalisation policy initiated in 1991, the Government of India has taken several measures to encourage foreign investment, both direct and portfolio, in almost all sectors of the economy. However, the emphasis has been on foreign direct investment (FDI) inflows in the: (a) development of infrastructure, (b) technological upgradation of Indian industry (c) projects having the potential for creating employment opportunities on a large scale and (d) setting up special economic zones and establishing manufacturing units therein. With a vast reservoir of skilled and cost-effective manpower, India is now recognized as one of the most attractive investment destinations by reputed international rating organisations.

Promotion of foreign direct investment forms an integral part of India's economic policies. The role of foreign direct investment in accelerating economic growth is by way of infusion of capital, technology and modern management practices. Government has put in place a liberal and transparent foreign investment regime where most activities are opened to foreign investment on automatic route without any limit on the extent of foreign ownership.

FDI, being a non-debt capital flow, is a leading source of external financing, especially for the developing economies. It not only brings in capital and technical know-how but also increases the competitiveness of the economy. Overall, it supplements domestic investment, much required for sustaining the high growth rate of the country. In recent years, significant changes have been made in the FDI policy regime by the Government to ensure that India becomes an increasingly attractive and investor-friendly destination.

Under the current policy regime, there are three broad entry options for foreign direct investors: (a) in a few sectors, FDI is not permitted (negative list), (b) in another small category of sectors, foreign investment is permitted only till a specified level of foreign equity participation and (c) in all other sectors, foreign investment up to 100 percent of equity participation is allowed. The third category has two subsets— one consisting of sectors where automatic approval is granted for FDI (often foreign equity participation less than 100 percent) and the other consisting of sectors where prior approval from the Foreign Investment Promotion Board (FIPB) is required.

FDI Approval Routes

Investments can be made by non-residents through the automatic route or the Government route. Under the automatic route, the non-resident investor or the Indian company does not require any approval from Government of India for the investment. Under the Government route, prior approval of the Government of India is required. Proposals for foreign investment under Government route are considered by FIPB.

Automatic Route: Companies proposing foreign investment under the automatic route do not require any government approval, provided the proposed foreign equity is within the specified ceiling and the requisite documents are filed with the RBI within 30 days of receipt of funds. Post-facto filing of data relating to the investment made with the RBI is for record and data purposes. The automatic route encompasses all proposals where the proposed items of manufacture/activity does not require an industrial licence and is not reserved for the small-scale sector.

The automatic approval route of the RBI was introduced to facilitate FDI inflows. However, during the post-policy period, the actual investment flows through the automatic route of the RBI against total FDI flows remained rather insignificant. This was partly due to the fact that crucial areas like electronics, services and minerals were left out of the automatic approval route. Another limitation was the ceiling of 51 percent on foreign equity holding. An increasing number of proposals were cleared through the FIPB route while the automatic approval route was relatively unimportant. However, since 2000 automatic approval route has become significant and accounts for a large part of FDI flows.

Government Approval: For the following categories, government approval for FDI through the Foreign Investment Promotion Board (FIPB) is necessary:
1. Proposals attracting compulsory licensing.
2. Items of manufacture reserved for the small scale sector.
3. Acquisition of existing shares.

FIPB ensures a single-window approval for the investment and acts as a screening agency (for sensitive/negative list sectors). FIPB approvals (or rejections) are normally received in 30 days. Some foreign investors use the FIPB application route where there may be absence of stated policy or lack of policy clarity.

Guidelines have been issued for establishment of Indian companies/transfer of ownership or control of Indian companies, from resident Indian citizens to non-resident entities. In sectors/activities with caps—including, inter alia, defence production, air transport services, ground handling services, asset reconstruction companies, private sector banking, broadcasting, commodity exchanges, credit information companies, insurance, print media, telecommunications and satellites—Government approval/FIPB approval is required in all cases where:

1. An Indian company is being established with foreign investment and is owned by a non-resident entity or;
2. An Indian company is being established with foreign investment and is controlled by a non-resident entity or;
3. The control of an existing Indian company—currently owned or controlled by resident Indian citizens and Indian companies, which are owned or controlled by resident Indian citizens—will be/is being transferred/passed on to a non-resident entity as a consequence of transfer of shares and/or fresh issue of shares to non-resident entities through amalgamation, merger/demerger, acquisition etc. or;
4. The ownership of an existing Indian company—currently owned or controlled by resident Indian citizens and Indian companies, which are owned or controlled by resident Indian citizens—will be/is being transferred/passed on to a non-resident entity as a consequence of transfer of shares and/or fresh issue of shares to non-resident entities through amalgamation, merger/demerger, acquisition etc.

These guidelines do not apply to sectors/activities where there are no foreign investment caps, that is, 100 percent foreign investment is permitted under the automatic route.

Further, foreign investment includes all types of foreign investments, i.e. FDI—investment by FIIs, NRIs, ADRs, GDRs, Foreign Currency Convertible Bonds (FCCBs) and fully, mandatorily and compulsorily convertible preference shares/debentures.

As already noted, FDI in a particular industry may, however, be made through: (a) the automatic route under powers delegated to the RBI or (b) with the approval accorded by the FIPB. The automatic route means that foreign investors only need to inform the RBI within 30 days of bringing in their investment and again within 30 days of issuing any shares. Companies getting foreign investment approval through FIPB route do not require any further clearance from RBI for the purpose of receiving inward remittance and issue of shares to foreign investors.

RBI has granted general permission under FEMA in respect to proposals approved by the FIPB. Such companies are, however, required to notify the concerned regional office of the RBI of receipt of inward remittances within 30 days of such receipts and again within 30 days of issue of shares to the foreign investors.

Foreign Investment Promotion Board (FIPB)

FIPB is the nodal agency for consideration of all proposals requiring prior government approval.

Levels of Approvals for Cases under Government Route: The Minister of Finance who is in-charge of FIPB considers the recommendations of FIPB on proposals with total foreign equity inflow of and below ₹ 1,200 crore.

The recommendations of FIPB on proposals with total foreign equity inflow of more than ₹ 1,200 crore are placed for consideration of Cabinet Committee on Economic Affairs (CCEA).

The CCEA considers proposals which may be referred to it by the FIPB/Minister of Finance (in-charge of FIPB).

Cases Which do not Require Fresh Approval: Companies may not require fresh prior approval of the Government, i.e. Minister in-charge of FIPB/CCEA for bringing in additional foreign investment into the same entity, in the following cases:

1. Entities the activities of which had earlier required prior approval of FIPB/CCFI/CCEA and which had, accordingly, earlier obtained prior approval of FIPB/CCFI/CCEA for their initial foreign investment but subsequently such activities/sectors have been placed

under automatic route.

2. Entities the activities of which had sectoral caps earlier and which had, accordingly, earlier obtained prior approval of FIPB/CCFI/CCEA for their initial foreign investment but subsequently such caps were removed/increased and the activities placed under the automatic route; provided that such additional investment along with the initial/original investment does not exceed the sectoral caps.

3. Additional foreign investment into the same entity where prior approval of FIPB/CCFI/CCEA had been obtained earlier for the initial/original foreign investment due to certain requirements and prior approval of the Government under the FDI policy is not required for any other reason/purpose.

FDI Inflows in Post-liberalization Period

India's Share in FDI Flows to Developing Countries: Available data suggest that the share of India in FDI flows to developing countries is meagre. In spite of the fact that India is a strategic location with access to a vast domestic and South Asian market, its share in world's total flow of direct investment hovers around 2 percent. India might remain high in the rankings as a favoured economy for FDI by MNCs, but it has been bypassed in favour of more attractive destinations like China and neighbouring countries in Southeast Asia. China remains on top as an FDI destination attracting more than half of the total FDI flows to developing Asian economies.

The current scenario calls for further liberalisation of norms for investment by present and prospective foreign entrepreneurs. Attracting foreign capital requires an investor-friendly environment. It underlines the need for efficient and adequate infrastructural facilities, availability of skilled and semi-skilled labour force, business-friendly public administration and moderate rates of taxation.

Annual Investment Inflows: The policy initiatives taken by the Government have catalysed investment as is evident from Table 3.1.

**Table 3.1: Trends in Foreign Investment Flows into India:
2001-02 to 2010-11**

Year	A. Direct Investment		B. Portfolio Investment		Total (A + B)	
	₹ crore	US$ million	₹ crore	US$ Million	₹ crore	US$ million
2001-02	29,235	6,130	9,639	2,021	38,874	8,151
2002-03	24,367	5,035	4,738	979	29,105	6,014
2003-04	19,860	4,322	52,279	11,377	72,139	15,699
2004-05	27,188	6,051	41,854	9,315	69,042	15,366
2005-06	39,674	8,961	55,307	12,492	94,981	21,453
2006-07	1,03,367	22,826	31,713	7,003	1,35,080	29,829
2007-08	1,40,180	34,835	1,09,741	27,271	2,49,921	62,106
2008-09	1,73,741	37,838	-63,618	-13,855	1,10,123	23,983
2009-10	1,79,059	37,763	1,53,516	32,376	3,32,575	70,139
2010-11	1,38,462	30,380	1,43,435	31,471	2,81,897	61,851

Source: RBI, *Handbook of Statistics on Indian Economy,* 2010-11, Table 155.

On a general basis, FDI inflows have almost consistently increased since 1991 while erratic pattern is noticeable in the case of portfolio investment.

Top Investing Countries: In terms of investing countries, Mauritius continues to account for the largest amount of FDI inflows. The special role of Mauritius is the consequence of special tax treatment accorded in India to investments routed through Mauritius. Singapore is at the second position with regard to FDI inflows followed by UK, Japan, US, and Netherlands. Foreign collaborations and FDI inflows received after the announcement of the New Industrial Policy in 1991 show that FDI inflows from Mauritius have risen substantially (Table 3.2).

Sectors Attracting Highest FDI Inflows: Since the initiation of the economic liberalisation process in 1991, the services sector and sectors such as housing and real estate, telecommunications, computer software and hardware, drugs and pharmaceuticals, chemicals, power, automobiles, and petro-chemicals have attracted considerable investments. In the changed investment climate, India offers exciting business opportunities in virtually every sector of the economy. Services sector and telecommunications are among the leading sectors attracting FDI (Table 3.3).

**Table 3.2 Share of Top 10 Investing Countries in
FDI Equity Inflows**

Country	Cumulative inflows (April 2000 to June 2012)		%age to total inflows (in terms of US$)
	₹ crore	US$ million	
1. Mauritius	2,97,189	65,608	38
2. Singapore	79,770	17,555	10
3. UK	76,846	16,314	9
4. Japan	59,785	12,663	7
5. USA	48,682	10,710	6
6. Netherlands	35,209	7,652	4
7. Cyprus	30,762	6,603	4
8. Germany	22,234	4,880	3
9. France	13,709	2,988	2
10. UAE	10,643	2,301	1
Total FDI Inflows	7,98,826	1,74,835	-

Source: Government of India, Ministry of Commerce and Industry, Department of Industrial Policy and Promotion, *India FDI Factsheet*, June 2012.

Opportunities for FDI Inflows in Indian

India has been ranked at the third place in global foreign direct investments in 2009 and will continue to remain among the top five attractive destinations for international investors during 2010-11, according to United Nations Conference on Trade and Development (UNCTAD) in a report on world investment prospects titled, 'World Investment Prospects

Survey 2009-2011' released in July 2009. The 2009 survey of the Japan Bank for International Cooperation released in November 2009, conducted among Japanese investors continues to rank India as the second most promising country for overseas business operations, after China A report released in February 2010 by Leeds University Business School, commissioned by UK Trade and Investment (UKTI), ranks India among the top three countries where British companies can do better business during 2012-14.

Table 3.3: Sectors Attracting Highest FDI Equity Inflows

Sector	Cumulative inflows (April 2000 to June 2012)		%age to total inflows (in terms of US$)
	₹ crore	US$ million	
1. Services sector	1,51,560	33,428	19
2. Construction activities	95,624	21,088	12
3. Telecommunications	57,120	12,560	7
4. Computer software & hardware	50,557	11,286	6
5. Drugs and Pharmaceuticals	45,313	9,659	6
6. Chemicals	39,236	8,116	5
7. Power	33,994	7,444	4
8. Automobile industry	31,929	6,965	4
9. Metallurgical industries	28,692	6,374	4
10. Petroleum and natural gas	26,676	5,139	3

Source: Government of India, Ministry of Commerce and Industry, Department of Industrial Policy and Promotion, *India FDI Factsheet*, June 2012.

According to Ernst and Young's 2010 European Attractiveness Survey, India was ranked as the 4th most attractive foreign direct investment (FDI) destination in 2010.

However, it is ranked the 2nd most attractive destination following China in the next three years. Moreover, according to the Asian Investment Intentions survey released by the Asia Pacific Foundation in Canada, more and more Canadian firms are now focussing on India as an investment destination. From 8 percent in 2005, the percentage of Canadian companies showing interest in India has gone up to 13.4 percent in 2010. The following section deals with the factors attracting the FDI Inflows to India.

Consumer Market

According to a study by the McKinsey Global Institute (MGI), 'Bird of Gold': The Rise of India's Consumer Market, Indian incomes are likely to grow three-fold over the next two decades and India will become the world's fifth largest consumer market by 2025, moving up from its 2007 position as the world's 12th largest consumer market. India ranks second in the Nielsen Global Consumer Confidence survey released on January 7, 2010—an indication that recovery from the economic downturn is faster in India with consumers more willing to spend. The survey showed that in addition to the emerging markets of Indonesia and India, eight of the top ten most confident markets in the fourth quarter of 2009 came from the Asia Pacific region. The Indian consumer will spend over ₹ 200 a day on average by the year 2025, steered by a ten-fold increase in the country's middle class population and a three-fold jump in household income during this period. According to a study by the McKinsey Global Institute, the aggregate consumer spending could more than quadruple to ₹ 70 trillion by 2025, from about ₹ 17 trillion in 2005.

FDI Performance of India and China

Despite enjoying healthy rates of economic growth, India and China have significant differences in their FDI performance. China continues to be a magnet of FDI flows and India's biggest competitor. China accounts for nearly half of the total FDI flows to developing Asian economies while India's share is only around 4 percent. FDI has contributed to the rapid growth of China's merchandise exports while FDI has been much less important in driving India's export growth. FDI in Indian manufacturing still remains domestic market-seeking. The difference in their FDI performance is attributable to basic determinants, development strategies and overseas networks.

On the basic economic determinants of inward FDI, China does better than India. China's total and per capita GDP are higher than India's, making it more attractive for market-seeking FDI. China has higher literacy and education rates, making it more attractive to efficiency-seeking investors. China has large natural resource endowments. In addition, China's physical infrastructure is more competitive, particularly in the coastal areas. However, India has an advantage in technical manpower, particularly in information technology. It also has better English language skills.

Some of the differences in competitive advantages of the two countries are illustrated by the composition of their inward FDI flows. China has become a key centre for hardware design and manufacturing by such companies as Acer, Ericsson, General Electric, Hitachi Semiconductors, Hyundai, Intel, LG Electronics, Microsoft, Mitac International Corporation, Motorola, Nokia, Philips, Samsung Electronics, Sony, Taiwan Semiconductor Manufacturing, Toshiba and other major electronics TNCs. India, on the other hand, specialises in IT services, call centres, business back-office operations and R&D.

Rapid growth in China has increased the local demand for consumer durables and non-durables such as home appliances, electronics equipment, automobiles, housing and leisure. This rapid growth in local demand, as well as competitive business environment and infrastructure, has attracted many market-seeking investors. It has also encouraged the growth of many local indigenous firms that support manufacturing.

Initiatives Needed for Attracting FDI into India

It is well known that FDI can complement local development efforts in a number of ways, including boosting export competitiveness; generating employment and strengthening the skills base; enhancing technological capabilities (transfer, diffusion and generation of technology); and increasing financial resources for development. It can also help plug a country in the international trading system as well as promote a more competitive business environment. In view of this, India should continue to take steps to ensure an enabling business environment to improve India's attractiveness as an investment destination and a global manufacturing hub. The following initiatives are needed to attract FDI in India.

Flexible Labour Laws: China gets maximum FDI in the manufacturing sector, which has helped the country become the manufacturing hub of the world and export more than US$ 400 billion per annum. The manufacturing sector can grow in India provided infrastructure facilities are improved, and labour reforms take off. The country needs to gradually move towards more flexible labour laws.

Relook at Sectoral Caps: Though the Government has hiked the sectoral cap for FDI over the years, it is time to revisit issues pertaining to limits in such sectors as coal mining, insurance, real estate, and retail trade, apart from the small-scale sector. Government should gradually put more sectors under automatic route for FDI. Bringing more sectors under the automatic route, increasing the FDI cap and simplifying procedural delays need to be addressed with more vigour. Various sops are provided to foreign investors setting up export-oriented units (EOUs), special economic zones (SEZs), or industrial and electronics hardware parks.

Though the SEZs in India are not as successful as in China, their performance has improved in recent years. However, there is an urgent need to improve these SEZs in terms of their size, road and port connectivity, assured power supply, flexible labour laws and decentralised decision-making. It is well known that China has been able to attract FDI due its trade promotion, particularly exports. In turn, FDI also helps exports and more than half of China's exports originate from 'FDI-owned' firms. The nexus between exports and FDI is well-documented. In fact, most developing countries such as China, Singapore, Korea and Malaysia boast of export-GDP ratios almost double that of India.

The Government needs to act on the promises made in the Trade Policy to reduce procedural hassles and make all export procedures online. This would certainly improve the FDI flow into the export-oriented industries. On the fiscal sops to investment, it is time to think about redesigning the incentives given on the basis of differential development of the places. Though the idea of developing backward areas by extending fiscal incentives to investors is good, investors are hardly likely to be interested in the backward areas. Much of the Chinese FDI comes to the developed coastal areas. Thus, giving fiscal incentives for investing in the backward areas has not been very successful, and the Government needs to change tack.

Good Governance: Improving governance and overall accountability in public office will not only help attract more FDI but also increase domestic investment. Given the economy's performance in the recent past and the recognition that India is one of the major emerging markets, the Government should try to improve the investment climate. Improved infrastructure, flexible labour laws and easy procedures are crucial to drawing more FDI. The recent literature on FDI also suggests that the quality of governance is a major positive for higher investment and growth. Therefore, a smart government, not big or small, is the key.

Conclusion

As far as the economic interpretation of the model is concerned; the size of the domestic market is positively related to foreign direct investment. The greater the market, the more customers and more opportunities to invest. Since FDI is mostly in the form of physical investment, investors would prefer the markets with better infrastructure. The attractiveness of the host market also affects the FDI positively and significantly. In many ways India's principal problem remains that of boosting its rate of saving and investment from the current about 23 percent of GDP to over 30 percent of GDP in order to make growth prospects take a quantum jump and become comparable with the high growth phases of the Chinese and East Asian economies. FDI becomes important in its own right if it makes contributions towards technology progress; productivity spillovers and consolidating niche export markets.

References

Aradhna Aggarwal (2008), Regional Economic Integration and FDI in South Asia: Prospects and Problems, *Indian Council for Research on International Economic Relations*, Working paper 218, July 2008.

Business World (2010), China, India Top FDI Destinations Till 2012, *ECONOM, Business World,* 07 September 2010.

Dirk Willem te Velde (2002), Policy Challenges for Sub-Saharan African Countries, *Overseas Development Institute*, 2002.

George Hoguet, India vs. China: Which is the Better Long-term Investment?, *ssga.com*.

Government of India (2012), Fact Sheet on Foreign Direct Investment (FDI), *Department of Industrial Policy and Promotion, Ministry of Commerce and Industry.*

Government of India (2002), Report of the Steering Group on Foreign Direct Investment, *Planning Commission*, GOI, New Delhi, 2002.

IMF (2009), World Economic Outlook: Crisis and Recovery. *International Monetary Fund*, 22 April, Washington, DC.

Klaus Schwab (2010), The Global Competitiveness Report 2010-2011, *World Economic Forum*, Geneva, Switzerland 2010.

KIEP Seminar (2003), India-South Korea Trade and Investment Relations, *www.kiep.go.kr.*

K.S. Chalapati Rao and Biswajit Dhar (2011), India's FDI inflows

Trends and Concepts. *Institute for Studies in Industrial Development*, ISID working paper 2011/01, New Delhi, February 2011.

Ministry of Commerce and Industry (2003), Manual on Foreign Direct Investment in India-Policy and Procedures, *Government of India*, New Delhi, May 2003.

Nirupam Bajpai, Nandita Dasgupta (2004), FDI to China and India: The Definitional Differences. *The Hindu*, May 15, 2004.

Pravakar Sahoo (2006), Why FDI eludes India, *Business Line*, 26, August 2006.

Julan Du, Mr. Yilu and Mr. Zhigang (China) (2008), FDI Location Choice: Agglomeration vs. Institutions, *International Journal of Finance and Economics*, Wiley Inter Science, International Journal of Finance and Economics 13: 2–107 (2008), Published online 13 September 2007.

Ramkishen S. Rajan, Sunil Rongala and Ramya Ghosh, Attracting Foreign Direct Investment (FDI) to India, *www.freewebs.com.*

RBI (2008), Indian Investment Abroad in Joint Ventures and Wholly-owned Subsidiaries: 2007-08 (April-March), *Reserve Bank of India*, July 2008.

Syed Khaja Safiuddin (2010), Foreign Direct Investment Inflows in India-Opportunities and Benefits, *Global Journal of Finance and Management*, Volume 2, Number 2 (2010), pp. 245-259.

Red Herring Staff (2007), China, India Still Top FDI Spots, *http://www.redherring.com,* December 2007.

UNCTAD (2009), Assessing the Impact of the Current Financial and Economic Crisis on Global FDI Flows, New York and Geneva, United Nations.

UNCTAD, World Investment Report, 2009, New York and Geneva, United Nations.

UNCTAD (2008a), World Investment Prospects Survey, 2008-2010, New York and Geneva, United Nations.

UNCTAD (2008b), World Investment Report 2008: Transnational Corporations and the Infrastructure Challenge. New York and Geneva, United Nations.

UNCTAD (2007), World Investment Prospects Survey, 2007-2009, New York and Geneva, United Nations.

United Nations Conference on Trade and Development (2009), World Investment Prospects Survey, 2009-2011, United Nations, New York and Geneva, 2009.

Zhou Siyu (2010), China Remains to FDI Destination, *China Daily*, September 09, 2010.

Websites
http://business.mapsofindia.com/fdi-india
http://www.indiadaily.com/editorial/16083.asp
http:/indiabudget.nic.in
http://www.steelonthenet.com
http://www.ibef.org
http://business.mapsofindia.com
http://alternativeperspective.blogspot.com/
http://www.uscc.gov
http://www.economywatch.com
http://en.reingex.com

4

FDI, Technology Transfer and Economic Growth

Pramila Singh and D.C. Gupta

FDI and Modern Growth Theory

The relationship between FDI and traditional growth theory is rather simple. In the traditional 'production function' approach pioneered by Solow (1956), long-run growth can only result from advances in technological knowledge. Without technological progress, diminishing marginal returns to both domestic and foreign investment would eventually limit economic growth. An exogenous increase in investment, whether from home or abroad, would increase the amount of capital (and output) per person, but this would only be temporary as diminishing returns would impose a limit to this growth. The implication for the global economy is that foreign investment can only offset this limit if it includes the transfer of new technological knowledge in the form of new goods, new markets or new processes Policies to attract foreign investment would only have a transitory effect on growth, unless they include incentives to encourage innovation.

In endogenous growth theory, FDI can affect growth in different ways. Most endogenous growth models focus on the production and use of new knowledge in the presence of increasing returns, non-convexities and monopoly power including a technology parameter that recognizes new ideas in the form of research and development (R&D) and human capital. As a technology parameter, foreign investment can generate growth and increasing returns through global knowledge transfers and domestic knowledge spillover and through these knowledge transfers, the theory predicts that foreign investment will increase the stock of knowledge by creating new products and processes, introducing new management practices and organizational arrangements, and improving the skills of the labour force. Even without majority ownership, foreign investment can lead to knowledge spillovers through minority JVs and licensing.

While Rebelo (1991) demonstrates that it is not necessary to assume diminishing returns to physical capital to generate economic growth, most endogenous growth models offset the negative feedback by including various externalities associated with increasing returns into the production function. The models of Romer (1986) and Lucas (1988) suggest that growth rates differ because the positive feedback generated by technological learning external to the firm (diffusion) may exceed the negative feedback engendered by diminishing marginal returns internal to the firm. Romer (1986) introduces a technology parameter in the production function that exhibits increasing returns to knowledge and constant returns in knowledge accumulation. This allows the model to generate growth through learning-by-doing and knowledge spillovers.

Technical knowledge is generally public (or non-rival) and at least partly excludable, tacit knowledge is private or firm-specific (rival) and is excludable in that it requires certain rights to access it. The main interest of the firm, therefore, is to enforce these rights to gain monopoly profits, yet for society it is the inability of the firm to protect these rights that may lead to certain 'positive externalities' or 'knowledge spillovers' that can offset the marginal diminishing returns to physical capital. FDI can play an important role in facilitating these knowledge spillovers across national boundaries, but this will depend not only on obtaining the right to use the technical knowledge and the ability to transfer tacit knowledge from the parent firm to the subsidiary. If individuals possess this knowledge as Lucas (1988) suggests, then human capital is a rival good that can spill over as a result of a contractual arrangement between individual and firm or organization. In this context, foreign firms may be attracted to a country or region because of the high skill levels and potentially high growth rates. As a lead variable, inward FDI can close the technology gap and generate economic convergence in these models, but as a lag variable it is just as likely to widen the technology gap as to close it (Krugman and Venables, 1995).

The role of multinational activity in facilitating economic growth is perhaps better understood in Romer (1990). In this model, Romer generates growth through the creation of human capital, differing from Lucas in that it represents the endowment of human capital as the intensity of R&D. This model also suggests that research contains positive feedback that increases the variety of intermediate inputs by creating general knowledge and inducing the amount of human capital needed for subsequent innovations since the growth rate is an increasing function of the amount of human capital dedicated to R&D, the choice between production and research determines the pace of growth. Thus, an increase in the intensity of research generates growth through a cumulative rise in product innovation. This product differentiation reflects the increased specialization of labour across an increasing variety of activities, whether domestic or international. As the economy grows, producers introduce new intermediate goods that increase the productivity of labour and capital.

Aghion and Howitt (1992) and Grossman and Helpman (1991) generate growth in a similar way as Romer (1990) but consider technological progress as an improvement in the quality of existing producer products. Old technology becomes obsolete through the introduction of new technology. Grossman and Helpman (1991) represent this process as a quality ladder that firms climb depending on the stochastic nature of the R&D process. Firms obtain monopoly profits from the introduction of new producer goods that force lower quality goods to exit the market. Inter-temporal improvements in the quality of production goods imply that the market outcome may not be optimal, but they may lead to either a higher or lower growth rate than is socially optimal since the knowledge spillovers can appear as a positive or negative externality.

The inclusion of foreign investment and technology licensing into the model increases the range of factor endowments where price equalization is possible. International knowledge spillovers occur as firms with high technological capabilities and high factor prices find it profitable to locate or license high technology production to a country with lower capabilities and lower factor prices. Over time, the country with high technological capabilities may become a net importer of high-tech products, as the affiliates export their finished products home, but also receive additional income from increased licence fees and the repatriation of profits.

Endogenous growth models have attempted to incorporate various channels of technology transfer. Dollar and Wolff (1993) show that international R&D spillovers play a significant role in explaining productivity growth across industries. Coe and Helpman (1995) describe how trade flows can facilitate the transfer of technology through R&D spillovers. Building on the model of Romer (1990) and Grossman and Helpman (1991), this model shows that a country's total factor productivity depends not only on its own R&D activity, but also on the R&D activity of its trading partners. Keller (1998) shows, however, that randomly generated trade flows can lead to similar or even higher international spillover effects on productivity compared with using actual trade shares. The implication of this analysis is that other channels of technology transfer may describe R&D spillovers better than trade flows. Borensztein *et al.* (1998) develop and test an endogenous growth model in which FDI affects growth through the transfer of technology. Though not statistically significant, the results of the test show that FDI has a positive impact on economic growth and is dependent on the level of human capital in the host country.

Technology Gaps and FDI

Gerschenkron (1962) developed the idea that technological differences explain differences in growth rates and hence the possibility of catching-up and convergence. The size of the gap creates an opportunity for catching-up with the technology leader, but this opportunity will depend on whether the relatively backward country can successfully imitate the technological leader. Abramovitz (1989) developed this argument further by arguing that the realization of this opportunity for closing the technology gap depends not only on the relative backwardness of the region, but also on the 'social capability' of each individual country to absorb new technology from abroad. Abramovitz and David (1996, p. 50) define social capability as the 'attributes, qualities, and characteristics of people and economic organization that originate in social and political institutions' that influence economic behaviour.

These institutional arrangements may include the education system and the organization of firms of that country, but could be defined more specifically as technological capabilities or competencies. Backward countries, therefore, have the potentiality for generating growth more rapid than that of more advanced countries, provided their social capabilities are sufficiently developed to permit successful exploitation of technologies already employed by the technological leaders (Abramovitz, 1989).

The realization of this potential for central Europe to catch-up with the EU will depend both on the presence of social capabilities and the size of the technology gap.

Social capability also includes the absorptive capacity of firms to assimilate technical knowledge from abroad. This social capability appears as an externality in neoclassical endogenous growth theory and as a joint product in the classical growth theory (Parrinello, 1993). Romer (1990) and Grossman and Helpman (1991) include international knowledge spillovers by distinguishing between a purely 'local' or national good and a 'global' or international good, but leave out the cost of building an absorptive capacity. According to Cohen and Levinthal (1989, p. 569), an absorptive capacity is the 'firm's ability to identify, assimilate and exploit knowledge from the environment'. When a firm wants to apply knowledge transferred from technological spillovers, it must enter into a time-consuming and costly process of investing in its absorptive capacity if it wants to imitate or improve. In this context, the idea of absorptive capacity becomes a connecting device between the potential for catching- up (technological opportunities) and its realization (appropriability conditions). This later factor is a necessary condition for firms to have incentives to invest in learning.

It is possible to restate the approach of Abramovitz (1989) so that catching-up in its complex form is the outcome of the existing technology gap, social capability and a variety of independent causes. From this perspective, factors of technology transfer should be considered as partly independent of those governing potentiality itself, and partly as a reflection of national social capability, in this case the capability to absorb and effectively use and innovate imported technology. This is in sharp contrast to the growth literature where the issue of how technology transfer contributes to growth is of no concern. The very mechanics of growth, or how technological, social and other independent factors interact and contribute to divergence/convergence processes, are not of prime concern. However, from a technology transfer perspective it is the mechanics (or process) that is the main concern. The approach which tries to take into account the interaction of these factors is the so-called national systems of innovation approach (see Lundvall, 1992; Nelson, 1993; Edquist, 1997). However, this approach lacks a strong underlying theoretical basis (Radoevié, 1998).

Verspagen (1991) presents a simple (non-linear) bifurcation model that captures the essence of Abramovitz and describes how social capability and the size of the technology gap can influence the potential for catching-up. This model shows that the technology gap tends to close when a country has a high learning capability or low initial gap and tends to widen when a country has a low learning capability and high initial gap. International technology spillovers will increase in the catching-up economies and then decrease slowly until there is some convergence of technology levels. Complete convergence occurs as the economy moves from an imitator to innovator and increases the domestic R&D levels up to a level comparable with the technological leader. FDI can potentially play an important role in facilitating the knowledge spillovers and increase the likelihood that the economy will bifurcate into the 'convergence club'.

Developing the capability to absorb new technologies was essential in every case of catching-up this century. Empirical studies show that few countries have these technological capabilities. 'While the developed OECD countries have been converging over time, Baumol (1986) shows that these groups of countries have also tended to grow faster than the world economy. Barro and Sala-i-Martin (1995) argue that the only convergence that occurs is so- called conditional convergence, by which they mean convergence after controlling for differences in steady states or situations in which a limited set of growth-related variables grow at a constant rate. The further an economy is below its steady state, the faster it should grow and vice versa; the further an economy is above its steady state, the slower the economy should grow (Jones, 1998). This suggests that the economic growth is a much more complex country-specific process, not easily amenable to generalizations.

The technology gap literature does not deal explicitly with technology transfer issues mainly for methodological reasons. This would require modelling a process with institutional variables in a dynamic context. While evolutionary modelling has made considerable progress in the last few years, it still has not reached a sufficient level to encompass the co-evolution of institutions and technologies. Moreover, it is difficult to separate the technology transfer from endogenous capability-building. Dunning (1994) has started to conceptualize the dual role they may play in the virtuous and vicious cycles of increasing and decreasing technological capability. Solvel and Zander (1995) point out that a common perspective in the new models is that the FIEs build increasingly complex organizational structures and management processes which allow technological learning and development across national borders. In that respect they function as a 'global learning vehicle'. However, taking into account the diversity of transfer channels and the different forms in which technology appears, it is probable that conceptualizations which link the catching-up process with technology transfer will remain very limited and vague.

Finally, the technology gap approach of Abramovitz (1989) and Verspagen (1991) shows how complex such an attempt would be. An alternative approach to analysing links between transfer and growth is to reduce it to measuring the costs and benefits in the host economy. We analyse this approach in the next two sections, which focus mainly on FDI. Other forms of technology transfer, like sub-contracting and alliances, are far more difficult to analyse as the technology content is implicit in these arrangements.

Economic Progress through FDI and Technology Transfer

The development literature of the 1960s and 1970s did not consider FDI as the best channel for growth and catching-up. Generally the share of equity capital that a foreign firm could own was often restricted because of the belief that equity relationships contained greater social costs than benefits. An assumed inverse relationship between the costs of transfer and the degree of foreign ownership led to a hierarchical ranking of channels according to their assumed benefit for a recipient. JVs were preferred over majority FDI, licensing over JVs and direct purchase over licensing. Hoffman and Girvan (1990) argue that an implicit assumption in the literature was that suppliers willing to agree to non-equity relationships would be smaller in size and have less bargaining power than FIEs, and, therefore, would agree to less costly contractual terms.

This hierarchy goes from less packaged towards more packaged forms of technology transfer, neglecting informal channels and alliances. Also, channels are seen as excluding each other. The absolute level of licensing is negatively related to the level of FDI so that these two strategies are seen as substitutes rather than complements. On the other hand, the rise of alliances shows the complementary rather than substitutive relationship among channels (Mowery and Oxley, 1995). The mainstream view in the literature on technology transfer is that unbundling the technology package is preferable to obtaining it bundled at a premium price. Ernst and O'Connor (1990) conclude that this may mean choosing a licence rather than joint ventures. Pack and Kamal (1997) also argue that licensing should generally be preferred to FDI even if it is hedged with some restrictions.

However, they all place certain reservations on this view. Contractor (1985) shows that technology licensing can be disadvantageous for a seller and advantageous for a buyer, if measured in terms of the net technology margin. Ernst and O'Connor (1990) point out that unbundling and licensing a particular technology may reduce the costs of acquisition, but it may raise absorption (learning) costs if the licensee does not have sufficient internal expertise. Finally, empirical evidence suggests that the technologies transferred to foreign affiliates are newer than those for outside licensing and joint ventures (Mansfield and Romeo, 1980).

There are two explanations for why differences in technology transfer channels may be of secondary importance in the literature. The first argument focuses on the ability of firms to successfully absorb the new technology. Technological benefits gained from foreign technology depend less on the method selected for the transfer than on how the method is implemented—especially with regard to building a firm's technological capabilities. There is evidence that there are small differences in transfer conditions between FIEs and domestic-owned firms. Based on research into 47 technology transfers from the UK to India, Alam and Langrish (1981) suggest that there is no significant difference in the conditions of transfer (sophistication, royalty, import) between FIEs and domestic- owned firms. However, while this evidence suggests that technology transfer channels are of secondary importance, these studies tend to neglect the role of policy and the firm in facilitating technology diffusion. Dahlman et al. (1987, p. 768) concludes, therefore, that 'the technological benefits to be gained from foreign technology depend less on the method selected for the transfer; more on how the method is implemented'.

The second explanation focuses on the impossibility to differentiate between the relative success and failure of different technology transfer channels. Examining the effectiveness of different channels oil countries' aggregate performance, Mowery and Oxley (1995) conclude that the mix of channels through which an economy obtains technology from foreign sources appears to be less important than the overall effort to exploit foreign sources of technology. Mowery and Oxley (1995) also suggest that channels alone are far from sufficient to explain the dynamic effects of technology transfer on the host economy. The secondary importance of technology transfer channels might be particularly pronounced at a macro-level, especially in high-growth economies, as the increasing absorptive capacity of these economies plays down all the factors which are seemingly important in a static framework (primarily costs), and the main concern of firms and policy makers is with the dynamic potential of specific technologies, irrespective of short-term costs.

Stewart (1981), Antonelli and Perosino (1992) and Vernon

(1986) suggest that it is difficult to reach definite conclusions regarding technology transfer mechanisms. As Stewart (1981) states, 'there are many factors that contribute to the overall breakdown, including recipient country policy, industrial composition, country source of supplies, etc.' The choice of channels contains specific firm, industry and country elements that are difficult to ignore. This mixture of firm, industry and country-specific factors playing a role in the selection of technology transfer channels is confirmed also by several empirical researches. Reddy and Zhao (1990) identify several factors in choosing the method of transferring technology: the competition faced by the supplier firm; the age of. the transferred technology; the nature of the transferred technology; and the importance of the technology to the supplier firm. Cortes and Bocock (1984) found that the type of product, and the country characteristics of both the recipient and supplier were important determinants of technology transfer in the Latin American petrochemicals industry Davidson and McFetridge (1993) found close relationships between the mode of transfer and the characteristics of the technology, the parent firm and certain demographic and geographic characteristics of receiving countries. There was a looser relationship between the mode of transfer and selected public policies of the receiving countries and no relationship at all between transfer mode and the economic characteristics of receiving countries.

The notion of different transfer mechanisms relate to corporate governance mechanisms. The proposition that we introduce is that intra-industry modes of governance determine typical technology transfer channels. For example, it is difficult to expect that in the textile industry, where the dominant governance mode is an arm's-length relationship, FDI might be the dominant technology transfer channel. Similarly, in the aviation industry it is difficult to expect that licences could be the dominant technology transfer mode. As Hollingsworth (1993) points out, modes of governance are contingent on markets, technology and customer characteristics, with markets being a cyclical component and technology and demand a long-term, structural component. On that basis, he developed a taxonomy of governance modes consisting of hierarchies, obligational networks (subcontracting and cooperative alliances) and markets.

Pavitt (1984) shows how technology transfer can be industry- and technology-specific. In supplier-dominated sectors technology mainly comes already embodied in production machines. In production-intensive sectors, key technologies relate to constructing and operating large-scale plants and are transferred internationally mainly through know-how agreements. In sectors supplying production equipment, technology is transferred internationally mainly through 'reverse engineering' and through local linkages with the production engineering departments in production-intensive user firms. In science-based firms the key technology emerges mainly from industrial R&D and in some cases from academic research. In information-intensive sectors (finance, retailing, publishing, travel), the technology transfer channel is purchase of equipment and software and 'reverse engineering'.

Static Effects of Multinational Activity

If the private costs and benefits to technology exporters were the same as the social costs and benefits to host countries, any form of technology import would automatically provide the right kind of technology for the host country. Benefits would outweigh costs if the social rate of return from inward investment (equal to the value-added less profit accruing to the foreign owners) is greater than the opportunity cost of the resources used. Dunning (1994) outlined the different costs and benefits that FDT has on the competitiveness and growth of the firm. He identified at least eight potential benefits from inward foreign direct investment:

1. Additional resources and technological capabilities.
2. New entrepreneurship, management styles and work

cultures.
3. Spillover effects in the domestic economy.
4. Effective demand.
5. Tax revenue.
6. Improving balance of payments through export growth and import substitution.
7. Access to global network.
8. Corporate governance.

He also identified at least seven cost factors that can offset these benefits:
1. Wrong kind of resources and assets.
2. Inability to adapt to local customs and culture.
3. Lock-in to low innovative dynamism.
4. Transfer pricing.
5. Worsening the balance of payments.
6. Abuse of power.
7. The global interests of the multinational may be inconsistent with the dynamic competitive advantage.

Costs and benefits are never confined only to enterprises involved in technology transfer; they spill over into other enterprises and other sectors. The costs and benefits of FDI or licences are augmented by those of suppliers of capital equipment and intermediary products to the foreign affiliates or domestic producers. This undoubtedly makes the calculation of costs and benefits rather complex. Even if it is possible to resolve the problems of measurement, time horizon and choice of discount rate, the problem of the dynamic potential of transfer, which is not reflected in current costs and benefits, remains. The dynamic potential of transfer is unknown because it is highly dependent on the domestic generation of knowledge. That is the primary reason why similar policies of technology transfer usually produce rather different results in different countries. A country may acquire, at high cost, a wide range of technological capabilities in different sectors, yet these will not necessarily result in augmented innovative capability.

In view of these problems, it is perhaps not surprising that none of the studies on technology transfer to developing countries have come up with satisfactory estimates of direct costs. Hoffman and Girvan (1990) identify four direct costs associated with technology transfer:

1. Direct costs.
2. Costs resulting from restrictions on the recipient's production and marketing.
3. Indirect costs associated with repatriated profits.
4. Costs associated with the purchase of inputs from suppliers.

Direct costs are charges for the right to patents, licences, know-how and trademarks (recurrent payments and lump-sum payments). It is assumed that direct costs on average amount to 2-5 percent for contracts using gross sales as a royalty base. Costs resulting from the restrictions on export and production are multiple and include contract obligations, restrictions on production, export restrictions, price fixing and the inefficient use of imported technology.

UNCTAD (1975) carried out the most systematic estimates of direct costs in the 1970s. They estimated that in 1968 the direct costs of technology transfer to developing countries were around US$ 1500 million in royalties and fee payments, equivalent to around 0.5 percent of GDP. Stewart (1981) estimated that technology payments were more than US$ 5 billion in 1977. IMF estimates for royalties were, as expected, far lower than those of UNCTAD (generally of the order of 0.5 percent to 1 percent of exports).

Stewart also assumed that tied purchase of capital goods added 30 percent to the costs of capital equipment, as may be suggested by the evidence on tied aid. So, for countries with around 75 percent of their inputs tied by technology contracts, the additional cost would be over 20 percent of the cost of capital equipment. Stewart (1981), states that the share of agreements containing such provisions in most countries is between 62 and 83 percent (1961), except in India where it was 15 percent (1961) and 5 percent (1964). On these grounds, Stewart justifies the significant foreign exchange savings that could be made by developing countries if they regulated technology imports.

There were no estimates of this kind carried out during the 1980s, except via the normal process of technology balance-of-payments statistics. An alternative approach to the issue of costs and benefits of technology transfer are cross-sectional studies which measure performance of domestic and foreign-owned affiliates. The assumption is that the higher labour productivity or more capital-intensive techniques or higher employment creation of foreign affiliates positively affects the host economy, including technology transfer. For example, Karake (1990) found, in the case of the Egyptian industrial sector, a positive and substantially larger impact from foreign than domestic technology, measured by marginal productivity of foreign capital. The analysis also revealed that the contribution of total factor productivity to output growth is small relative to the contribution of physical inputs.

Helleiner (1989) cites only two case studies that show reductions in the host country's national product in the presence of FDI. FDI lowered national income and welfare in the host country though it earned profits for the private foreign investor. He concludes that the incidence of bad FDI projects and lower social rates of return were systematically associated with higher levels of domestic protection against imports. Administratively determined input prices like subsidized energy also played a significant role in these results. His conclusion is that FDI has mostly generated positive economic effects for host countries.

Studies reviewed in UNCTAD (1997) suggest that foreign affiliates are often more efficient in production than their domestic counterparts. Labour productivity in foreign affiliates tended to be higher than that in domestic firms in the same industry. This review also recognized that in some cases these differences diminished when the data were controlled for size of firm, suggesting that the productivity differences observed relate to differences in capital intensity and scale as well as in technology, and organizational capabilities.

Jenkins (1990) suggests that evidence does not support any strong statement about the relative performance of FIEs and local firms. He ascribes this to the inherent limitations of cross-section studies which often failed to reveal any clear-cut general pattern. The implicit assumption of cross-section analysis is that the behaviour of local firms and foreign subsidiaries are independent of each other, and that there are differences between foreign and local firms which are universally valid. Jenkins goes on to suggest that a more fruitful approach is to be found in longitudinal studies. This approach would show that the behaviour between local and foreign firms is mutually dependent and that differences between them are often sector-, country- or technology-specific. This interaction creates dynamics which are difficult to reveal through cross-section analysis. Dunning (1993), points out that 'the dynamic view on technology transfer costs and benefits would bring out more clearly the trade-off between the wish to minimize real costs and to maximize technology contribution'.

Dynamic Effects of Multinational Activity

The main reason why countries attempt to attract foreign investment is the desire to obtain new technology. Even if multinational firms carry out foreign activity in wholly owned affiliates, technology is to some extent a public good. Benefits to the host economy can take the form of various externalities, or what is often called 'productivity' or 'technological' spillovers. In neoclassical economic theory, these spillovers are usually associated with market imperfections and the inability of firms to appropriate the full benefit of their own R&D activity in neoclassical theory.

The inability to protect this proprietary knowledge could either reduce business R&D activity is suggested by Nelson

(1959) and Arrow (1962) or increase it as Cohen and Levinthal (1989) maintain. By definition spillovers create a dichotomy between private and social returns. Bernstein and Nadiri (1988) define social returns as private rate plus the inter-industry marginal cost reductions due to spillovers. Technology spillovers are important if local firms are able to appropriate this public knowledge that foreign affiliates have generated. Subcontracting, competition and the labour market can play an important role in facilitating these spillovers, (Blomstrom and Kokko, 1998).

Mohnen (1990) identifies two general approaches to defining technology spillovers in the literature: (i) the spillover is an unweighted sum of the R&D stock of all other sectors in the economy or in the industry; and (ii) the spillover is a weighted sum of all the other R&D stock, with different proximity measures used to construct weights. Depending on the proximity measure used, Mohnen further distinguishes the weights proportional to the flows of intermediate purchase, to the flows of patents, or the flows of innovations between the sectors, or the correlation of the position vectors of these sectors in a technology space. In this last group the stock of each potential source of R&D spillover is entered separately into the production function.

Empirical analysis that follows the first approach initially estimated the social returns to a well-defined innovation, but later focused more on the effects spillovers have on productivity. In his pioneering work, Griliches (1958) calculated current and future consumer surplus flows, discounted them back to the present, and compared them to the cumulated research cost. Technology impact studies also used a similar methodological approach. If the imported technology is embodied in a domestic product or range of products, then it is possible to measure the social returns to the particular stream of imports by the sum of the product and consumer surplus generated by it. Private rates of return to R&D capital are the returns to the R&D performers, and social rates of return are the returns to the R&D users.

To demonstrate the extent of spillovers, Griliches shows that the social rate of return is several times greater than the private rate in almost all cases. Imported knowledge influences downstream industries through declining real factor prices, a pecuniary externality. It is more difficult, however, to measure the impact that knowledge flows have on productivity. This is a non-pecuniary externality that is not embodied in a particular service or product, though it may be covered by a licence. To measure these directly, it is necessary to assume either that their benefits are localized in a particular industry or range of products or that one can detect the path of spillovers. It is also necessary to consider the time lags in the realization of effects in other sectors, which always take more time than the direct effects of transfer.

The second approach to spillovers developed regress-based estimates of overall returns to a particular stream of outside R&D expenditures. These estimates relate R&D capital or R&D intensity (R&D to sales ratio or value added) to the growth rate of output or total factor productivity across firms or industries (Griiches, 1991). Spillovers appear in these models as the sum of current expenditures of firms or industries on R&D, the sum of R&D capital stock, R&D stock weighted by patents, or R&D desegregated according to each distinct potential spillover source (Bernstein, 1991).

Studies of developing countries suggest that spillovers can either complement or substitute domestic R&D activity. 'While there is little evidence as to the nature of spillovers, they can appear substantial both within and between industries, but they may also be insignificant or even non-existent (Mohnen, 1990; Blomstram and Kokko, 1998). The evidence on spillovers in multinational activity suggests that they are country-specific and often only in one direction. In a review of 12 studies from developed and developing countries, Dunning (1985) concluded that multinational affiliates had a beneficial effect on resource allocation at least in a static sense, although about half of the studies stressed that the beneficial effects might have been even greater with different government policies. Spillovers were positive in advanced industrial economies and in some sectors substantial, whereas in the smaller developed and less developed countries results were mixed. A study by Young *et al.* (1994) suggest that dynamic gains from multinational activity are mainly confined to acquired companies and in the form of improved availability of investment funds, and improved management and marketing skills. In some cases, such as Scotland, inward FDI may have reduced sub-contracting and corporate functions.

There are few direct analyses of the existence and significance of spillovers and most of them focus on the effects they have on the industrial structure. Early studies on Australia by Caves (1974), Canada by Globerman (1979) and Mexico by Blomström and Persson (1983) show that spillovers are significant at the industry level, but do not explain how they take place (Blomstrom and Kokko, 1998). A study by Kokko (1992) found that technology import and productivity levels of affiliates in Mexico appear to be positively related to the skills level of the host country's labour force, and the degree of competition from local firms, but negatively related to the existence of technology transfer and performance requirements.

Blomström and Wolff (1994) found that spillovers increased productivity growth of local firms and led to a convergence of Mexican productivity towards US levels from 1970 to 1975. Nadiri (1991) reaches a similar conclusion for France, Germany, Japan and the UK. By contrast, a study of Moroccan manufacturing from 1985 to 1989 by Haddad and Harrison (1993) shows that spillovers did not increase productivity growth of local firms because it took place mainly in sectors with simpler technology and not in the more knowledge-intensive industries. Mixed results were also found for Venezuela by Aitken and Harrison (1999).

Several case studies from East Asia also support the

existence of spillovers. Kim (1993) found that technology developed within electronic multinationals in Singapore and Malaysia spills over to their local suppliers and the labour market. Dahlman and Brimble (1990) show that foreign firms in Thailand have not developed significant linkages with local companies and have not generated positive spillover benefits in the areas of technical training or technology transfer to local firms. They offer limited technical assistance and quality control that normally accompany subcontracting arrangements. In addition, the training effect of foreign firms has been mainly felt at the level of direct shop-floor workers, with only isolated effects at the higher technical and management levels.

The evidence on spillovers reveals that individual country-, industry- and firm-specific factors influence the incidence of the spillovers. Bernstein (1991) analysed differences between Canadian-owned firms and affiliates and showed that there was a correlation between R&D activity and the spillover effects in different industries. In industries with high R&D propensity a complementary relationship exists between industry spillovers and R&D capital for both groups. The more spillover benefits they receive, the more they invest in R&D. An empirical study by Kokko (1994) suggests that spillovers are industry-specific. He found that factors related to technology alone do not appear to inhibit spillovers, but large productivity gaps and large foreign market shares together appear to make up significant obstacles.

In industries where the productivity gap in relation to foreign affiliates is high and where their market share is also high, we may expect that foreign affiliates operate in enclaves, which are isolated segments of the market where technologies, products and plant sites are very different from those used by local firms. Spillovers are not an automatic consequence of foreign investment and depend on market structures and various inducements to the industry.

Finally, UNCTAD (1997) points to the technological capabilities of local firms relative to those of foreign affiliates, and how their market strategies have an important influence on the incidence of the spillovers. All of these individual country-, industry- and firm-specific factors may cause considerable difficulty in any empirical analysis, as Jenkins (1990) keenly observed.

The existence of spillovers suggests that FDI affects growth endogenously through increasing returns generated in interaction between local firms and foreign affiliates. Spillovers depend on the features of firms, industries, countries, technologies and markets. The causality among these factors and spillovers is context-specific and generalizations are limited. Three policy conclusions emerge from the literature. First, there is no general policy for maximizing spillovers. Spillovers are sector-specific, and general incentives to maximize the indirect benefits from the presence of foreign FIEs may be highly effective in some sectors but have no effect in others. The overall benefit is dependent on a country's industry and market structure and general technological level.

Second, the spillovers are less likely in sectors where product differentiation and scale economies are strong. In these sectors the advantages of FIEs are greater and they can easily take over the whole domestic market. Kokko (1994) suggests that backward countries should try to attract FDI in sectors where these factors are not dominant. This policy could be undermined, however, because FIEs are less present in sectors they cannot exploit ownership-specific advantages in differentiated products and scale economies.

Third, spillovers are more likely in sectors where the productivity gap between local and foreign firms is not too high (Kokko, 1994; Pack and Kamal, 1997; UNCTAD, 1997). If the productivity gap between them is too high, local firms are not able to capture the benefits of possible spillovers. This suggests that P01 may create large benefits only above a certain development threshold as suggested in the model of Verspagen (1991).

Economic Restructuring through Technology Transfer

Historical analyses show that technology transfer, complemented with domestic technology accumulation, is essential to the growth process (Mokyr, 1990). Successful catching-up is most often based on extensive technology acquisition from the leaders. The industrialization in the nineteenth century of Germany, France and the USA relied on the transfer of knowledge from the UK. The catching-up of Japan in the 1960s and 1970s, and South Korea in the 1980s, also relied initially on imported technology from the West. The reason for this is that the costs of imitation and technology import are lower for followers than the cost of innovation for the leaders. Freeman and Soete (1997) point out that the use of imported foreign technology is not a straightforward short cut to technical change and technological learning. Effective assimilation of foreign technology is actually difficult and complex. Access to imported technology is far from sufficient for catching-up and the import of technology does not of itself generate technological dynamism unless it is accompanied by an active building up of domestic technology capability (Sandberg, 1992).

There is great optimism in central Europe that P01 can speed up the process of economic transformation. The reason is that FDI is both industry- and context-specific and there is no automatic mechanism to ensure a technology transfer. FDI affects growth endogenously and spillover effects cannot be understood out of a variety of country- and industry-specific factors.

FDI is not the only channel of technology transfer into central Europe. The effects of FDI are complementary to various other forms of co-operation including trade, subcontracting and other types of alliance networks. Both the direct and indirect effects of FDI should be seen in the context of other technology transfer channels. This creates certain difficulties, however, since data on the technology composition of trade and subcontracting do not exist for central Europe. However, it is clear in the literature that there is no general policy for maximizing technology spillovers. The legislation in central Europe implicitly accepts this view in that it gives foreign enterprises the same status as domestic firms and provides certain incentives for FDI.

References

Abramovitz, M. (1989), Thinking About Growth, Cambridge: Cambridge University Press.

Abramovitz, M. and P.A. David (1996), 'Convergence and deferred catch-up: productivity leadership and the waning of American exceptionalism', in R. Landau, R. Taylor and O. Wright (eds.), the Mosaic of Economic Growth. Stanford: Stanford University Press, pp. 21-62.

Aghion, P. and P. Howitt (1992), 'A model of growth through creative destruction', Econometrica.

Aitken, B.J. and A.E. Harrison (1999), 'Do domestic firms benefit from direct investment. Evidence from Venezuela', American Economic Review, 89, pp. 605-18.

Alam, G. and Langrish (1981), 'Non-multinational firms and transfer of technology to less developed countries', World Development, 4.

Antonelli, C. and G. Perosino (1992), 'Technology transfer revisited', FAST Programme mimeo, June.

Arrow, K. (1962), 'Economic welfare and the allocation of resources for invention', in The Rate and Directions of Inventive Activity: Economic and Social Factors, Princeton: Princeton University Press, pp. 609-626.

Barro, K. and X. Sala-i-Martin (1995), Economic Growth, New York: McGraw-Hill.

Baumol, W.J. (1986), 'Productivity growth, convergence and welfare —what the long run data show', American Economic Review, 76, pp. 1072-1075.

Bernstein, I. J. (1991), 'R&D capital, spillovers and foreign affiliates in Canada', in D. McFetridge (ed.), Foreign Investment, Technology and Economic Growth, Calgary: University of Alberta Press, pp. 111-112.

Bernstein, Ii and M.I. Nadiri (1988), 'Inter-industry R&D spillovers, rates of return, and production in high-tech industries', American Economic Review, 78, pp. 429-434.

Blomstrom, M. and A. Kokko (1998), 'Multinational corporations and spillovers', Journal of Economic Systems, 12, pp. 247-277.

Bloniström, M. and H. Persson (1983), 'Foreign investment and spillover efficiency in an underdeveloped economy: evidence from the Mexican manufacturing industry', World Development, 11, pp. 493-501.

Blomstrom, M. and B. Wolff (1994), 'Foreign investment enterprises and productivity convergence in Mexico', in W Baumol, K. Nelson and E. Wolff (eds), C'onvergence of Productivity: Cross-national Studies and Historical Evidence, Oxford University Press, pp. 263-284.

Borensztein, B., I Dc Gregorio, J-W Lee (1998), 'How does foreign direct investment affect growth?', Journal of International Economics, 45, pp. 115-135.

Caves, R.E. (1974), 'Multinational firms, competition and productivity in host- country markets', Economica, 41, pp. 176-193.

Coe, T.D. and U. Helpman (1995), 'International R&D spillovers', European Economic Review, 39, pp. 859-887.

Cohen, WM. and D.A. Levinthal (1989), 'Innovation and learning: the two faces of R&D', Economic Journal, 99, pp. 569-596.

Contractor, FT. (1985), 'Licensing vs. direct foreign investment in US corporate strategy: an analysis of aggregate US data', in N. Rosenberg and C. Frischtak (eds.), International Technology Transfer Concepts, Measures, and Comparisons, New York: Prager, pp. 277-320.

Cortes, M. and P. Bocock (1984), North-South Technology Transfer a Case Study of Petrochemicals in Latin America, Washington, DC: World Bank.

Dahlman, C. I. (1979), 'The problem of externality', Journal of Law and Economics, 22, p. 141.

Dahlman, C.I and P. Brimble (1990), 'Technology strategy and policy for industrial competitiveness: a case study in Thailand', Industry and Energy Department Working Papers, No. 24, Washington, DC: World Bank.

Dahlman, CT., B. Ross-Larsonn and L. Westphal (1987), 'Managing technological development: lessons from the newly industrializing countries', World Development, 15, pp. 759-775.

Davidson, W. H. and D. McFetridge, (1993), 'The choice of international technology transfer', in C.S. Nagpal and A.C.

Mittal (eds.), International Technology Transfer, New Delhi: Anmol Publications.

Dollar, D. and E. Wolff (1993), Competitiveness, Convergence, and International Specialization, Cambridge: MIT Press.

Dunning, III. (1985), Multinational Enterprise, Economic Structure and International Competitiveness, New York: Wiley.

Dunning, IH. (1994), 'Re-evaluating the benefits of foreign direct investment', Transnational Corporations, 3, pp. 23-51.

Edquist, C. (ed.) (1997), Systems of Innovation, Technologies Institutions and Organizations, London: Pinter.

Ernst, D. and D. O'Connor, (1990), Technology and Global Competition: the Challenges for Newly Industrializing Economies. Development Centre, Paris: OECD.

Freeman, C. and L. Soete (1997), The Economics of Industrial Innovation, 3rd edn, London: Pinter.

Gerschenkron, A. (1962), Economic Backwardness in Historical Perspective, Cambridge: Harvard University Press.

Globerman (1979), 'Foreign direct investment and "spillover" efficiency benefits in Canadian manufacturing industries', Canadian Journal of Economics, 12, pp. 42-56.

Griliches, Z. (1958), 'Research costs and social returns: hybrid corn and related innovations', Journal of Political Economy, 66, pp. 919-931.

Griliches, Z. (1991), 'The Search for R&D Spillovers', NBER Working Paper, No. 3768.

Grossman, G. and E. Helpman (1991), Innovation and Growth in the Global Economy, Cambridge: MIT Press.

Grossman, G.M. and F. Helpman (1995), 'Technology and trade', in G. Grossman and K. Rogoff, Handbook of International Economics, Vol. III.

Helleiner, G.K. (1989), 'Transnational corporations and direct foreign investment', in H. Chenery and T.N. Srinivasan (eds.), Handbook of Development Economics II, Amsterdam: North Holland, pp. 1442-1480.

Hoffman, K. and N. Girvan (1990), 'Managing international technology transfer: a strategic approach for developing countries', mimeo MR 259e, IDRC, April.

Hollingsworth, R. (1993), 'Variation among nations in the logic of manufacturing sectors and international competitiveness', in D. Foray and C. Freeman (eds.), Technology and the Wealth of

Nations: The Dynamics of Constructed Advantages, London: Pinter.

Jenkins, R. (1990), 'Comparing foreign subsidiaries and local firms in LDCs: theoretical issues and empirical evidence', The Journal of Development Studies, 26, pp. 205-28.

Jones, C. I. (1998), Introduction to Economic Growth, New York: WW Norton.

Karake, A.Z. (1990), 'Technology transfer and economic growth in the less- developed countries: a technology gap approach', in M. Chatterji (ed.), Technology Transfer in Developing Countries, London: Macmillan.

Keller, W. (1998), 'Are international R&D spillovers trade related? Analyzing spillovers among randomly matched trade partners', European Economic Review, 42, pp. 1469-1481.

Kim, Y.C.L. (1993), 'Technology policy and export development: the case of electronics industry in Singapore and Malaysia', mimeo.

Kokko, A. (1992), 'Foreign direct investment, host country characteristics and slipovers', Ph.D. thesis, Stockholm School of Economics.

Kokko, A. (1994), 'Technology, market characteristics, and spillovers', Journal of Development Economics, 43, pp. 279-293.

Krugman, P. and A. Venables (1995), 'Globalization and the inequality of nations', Quarterly Journal of Economics, 110, pp. 857-880.

Lucas, R.E. (1988), 'On the mechanics of economic development', Journal of Monetary Economics, 22, pp. 3-42.

Lundvall, B.A. (ed.) (1992), National Systems of Innovation: Towards a Theory of Innovation and Interactive Learning, London: Pinter.

Mansfield, E. and A. Romeo (1980), 'Technology transfer to overseas subsidiaries by US-based firms', Quarterly Journal of Economics, 95, pp. 737-750.

Mohnen, P. (1990), 'New technology and inter-industry spillovers', STI Review, 7, pp. 131-147.

Mokyr, I. (1990), The Lever of Riches: Technological Creativity and Economic Progress, New York: Oxford University Press.

Mowery, D. and J.E. Oxiey (1995), 'Inward technology transfer and competitiveness: the role of national innovation systems',

Cambridge Journal of Economics, 19, pp. 67-93.

Nadiri, M.I. (1991), 'Innovation and technological spillovers', mimeo, New York University.

Nelson, R.R. (1959), 'The simple economics of basic scientific research', Journal of Political Economy, 67, pp. 297-306.

Nelson, R.R. (1993), National Innovation Systems. A Comparative Analysis, Oxford: Oxford University Press.

Pack, H. and S. Kamal (1997), 'Inflows of foreign technology and indigenous technological development', Review of Development Economics, 1, pp. 81-98.

Parrinello, S. (1993), 'Non pure private goods in the economics of production processes', Metro economical, 44, pp. 195-214.

Pavitt, K. (1984), 'Sectoral patterns of technological change: towards a taxonomy and a theory', Research Policy, 13, pp. 343-373.

Radosevic, S. (1997a), 'Technology transfer in global competition: the case of economies in transition', in D.A. Dyker (ed.), The Technology of Transition: Science and Technology Policies for Transition Countries, Budapest: Central European University Press, pp. 126-158.

Radosevic, S. (1997b), 'The Baltic post-socialist enterprises and the development of organisational capabilities', in N. Hood et al. (ed.), Micro-level Studies of the Transition in the Baltic States, London: Macmillan, p. 1945.

Radosevic, S. (1998), 'Defining systems of innovation: a methodological discussion', Technology In Society, 20, pp. 75-86.

Rebello, S. (1991), 'Long-run policy analysis and long-run growth', Journal of Political Economy, 99, pp. 500-521.

Reddy, N.M. and L. Thao (1990), 'International technology transfer: a review', Research Policy, 19, pp. 285-307.

Romer, P.M. (1986), 'Increasing returns and long-run growth', Journal of Political Economy, 94, pp. 1002-1037.

Romer, P.M. (1990), 'Endogenous technological change', Journal of Political Economy, 98, S71-S102.

Sandberg, M. (1992), Learning from Capitalists: a Study of Soviet Assimilation of Western Technology, Goteborg: Almquist and Wirksell International.

Solow, R. (1956), 'A contribution to the theory of economic growth', Quarterly Journal of Economics, 70, pp. 65-94.

Solvell, 0. and I. Zander (1995), 'Organisation of the dynamic multinational enterprise: the home-based and the heterarchical MNE', International Studies of Management and Organisation, 25, pp. 17-38.

Stewart, F. (1981), 'International technology transfer: issues and policy option', World Development, pp. 67-110.

UNCTAD (1975), Major Issues Arising from the Transfer of Technology to Developing Countries, New York: United Nations.

UNCTAD (1997), World Investment Report J997: Transnational Corporations. Market Structure and. Competition Policy, New York: United Nations.

Vernon, R. (1986), 'The curious character of the international technology market: an economic perspective', in IR. Mcintyre and D.S. Papp (eds.), The Political Economy of International Technology Transfer, New York: Quorum Books, pp. 160-207.

Verspagen, B. (1991), 'A new empirical approach to catching up or falling behind', Structural Change and Economic Dynamics, 2, pp. 359-380.

5

Foreign Direct Investment in SAARC Countries

P. Srinivasan, M. Kalaivani and P. Ibrahim

Introduction

Foreign direct investment (FDI) is an investment involving a long-term relationship and reflecting a lasting interest and control by a resident entity in one economy (foreign direct investor or parent enterprise) in an enterprise resident in an economy other than that of the foreign direct investor (FDI enterprise or affiliate enterprise or foreign affiliate). Foreign direct investment implies that the investor exerts a significant degree of influence on the management of the enterprise resident in the other economy. Such investment involves both the initial transaction between the two entities and all subsequent transactions between them and among foreign affiliates; both incorporated and unincorporated. FDI may be undertaken by individuals as well as business entities (UNCTAD, 2000). Foreign direct investment (FDI) is widely viewed as an important catalyst for the economic transformation of the transition economies.

The most widespread belief among researchers and policy makers is that FDI boosts growth through different channels. It increases the capital stock and employment, stimulate technological change through technological diffusion and generate technological spillovers for local firms. As it eases the transfer of technology, foreign investment is expected to increase and improve the existing stock of knowledge in the recipient economy through labour training, skill acquisition and diffusion. It contributes to introduction of new management practices and more efficient organisation of the production processes, which in turn would improve productivity of host countries and stimulate economic growth. The advent of endogenous growth models (Romer, 1986, 1987; Lucas, 1988, 1990; and Mankiw, 1992) considered FDI contributes significantly to human capital such as managerial skills and research and development (R&D).

Multinational Corporations (MNCs) can have a positive impact on human capital in host countries through the training courses they provide to their subsidiaries' local workers. The training courses influence most levels of employees from those with simple skills to those who posses advanced technical and managerial skills. Research and development activities financed by MNCs also contribute to human capital in host countries and thus enable these economies to grow in the long term (Blomstrom and Kokko 1998; Balasubramanyam et al. 1996).

By and large, there is a direct relationship between inward foreign direct investment in relation to their size and economic development of a country. One of the strongest statements in that connection was made by Romer (1993) who suggested that for a developing country that wishes to gain on the developed countries, or at least keep up with their growth "...one of the most important and easily implemented policies to give foreign firms an incentive to close the idea gap, to let them make a profit from doing so...The government of a poor country can therefore help its residents by creating an economic environment that offers an adequate reward to multinational corporations when they bring ideas from the rest of the world and put them to use with domestic resources".

On the other hand, the FDI can exert a negative impact on economic growth of the recipient countries. The dependency school theory argues that foreign investment from developed countries is harmful to the long-term economic growth of developing nations. It asserts that First World nations became wealthy by extracting labour and other resources from the Third World nations. It also argued that developing countries are inadequately compensated for their natural resources and are thereby sentenced to conditions of continuing poverty. This kind of capitalism based on the global division of labour causes distortion, hinders growth, and increases income inequality in developing countries (Stoneman, 1975; Bornschier, 1980 and O'hearn, 1990).

Further, the neo-classical growth models of Solow (1956) typically ascribe negligible long-run growth effects for FDI inflows and, with its usual assumption of diminishing returns to physical capital, these inflows can only have short-run impacts on the level of income, leaving long-run growth unchanged. Moreover, FDI flows may have a negative effect on the growth prospects of a country if they give rise to substantial reverse flows in the form of remittances of profits and dividends and/or if the MNCs obtain substantial tax or other concessions from the host country. These negative effects would be further compounded if the expected positive spillover effects from the transfer of technology are minimized or eliminated altogether because the technology transferred is inappropriate for the host country's factor proportions (e.g., too capital intensive); or, when this is not the case, as a result of overly restrictive intellectual property rights and/or prohibitive royalty payments and leasing fees charged by the MNCs for the use of the "intangibles" (see Ramirez, 2000 and Ram and Zhang, 2002).

Review of Literature

From the above theoretical arguments, it appears that the debate of whether FDI inflows are growth-enhancing or growth-retarding in the emerging economies remains largely an empirical question. Considerable volume of research has been conducted on the subject, but still there exist conflicting evidences in the literature regarding the FDI-growth relationship. Early studies on FDI, such as Singer (1950), Prebisch (1968), Griffin (1970) and Weisskof (1972) supported the traditional view that the target countries of FDI receive very few benefits because most benefits are transferred to the multinational company's country. Bacha (1974) examined the effects of FDI by US companies on the host country's growth. Their results revealed a negative relationship between these two variables, while Saltz (1992) examined the effect of FDI on economic growth for 68 developing countries and he also found a negative correlation between FDI and growth.

Similarly, Haddad and Harrison (1993) and Mansfield and Romeo (1980) find no positive effect of FDI on the rate of economic growth in developing countries. As De Mello (1999) points out, "whether FDI can be deemed to be a catalyst for output growth, capital accumulation, and technological progress seems to be a less controversial hypothesis in theory than in practice" (1999, p. 148). In his study, De Mello (1999) used both time series and panel data from a sample of 32 developed and developing countries found weak indications of the causal relationship between foreign direct investment and economic growth. Similarly, other studies such as Carkovic and Levine (2002) for 72 developed and developing countries, Mencinger (2003) for 8 transition countries and Eric Fosu and Joseph Magnus (2006) for Ghana found that FDI has a negative impact on economic growth.

On the other hand, the empirical literature supports the modernisation view that foreign direct investment can exert a positive impact on economic growth in emerging economies. Using a single equation estimation technique with annual data over the period 1960-1985 for 78 developing countries, Blomstrom et al. (1992) showed a positive influence of FDI inflows on economic growth. In an empirical study by Borensztein et al. (1998), an endogenous growth model was developed that measures the influence of the technological diffusion of FDI on economic growth in 69 developing countries over two periods, 1970-1979 and 1980-1989. They found that FDI inflows positively influenced economic growth.

Moreover, the relationship between FDI and domestic

investment in these countries was complementary. Campos and Kinoshita (2002) examined the effects of FDI on growth for 25 Central and Eastern European and former Soviet Union economies. Their results indicated that FDI had a significant positive effect on the economic growth of each selected country. Besides, the other studies by Marwah and Tavakoli (2004) for ASEAN-4 countries, Lumbila (2005) for 47 African countries, Aghion et al. (2006) for 118 countries, Lensink and Morrissey (2006) for 87 countries, Feridun and Sissoko (2006) for Singapore and Har Wai Mun et al. (2008) for Malaysia revealed that FDI has a positive impact on GDP growth. Moreover, the recent study of Reyadh and Khalifa (2009) shows that, for most of the Gulf Cooperation Council (GCC) countries, there is a weak but statistically significant causal impact of FDI inflows on economic growth.

Some empirical studies indicate that higher economic growth will lead to greater FDI inflows into host countries. Jackson and Markowski (1995) had found that economic growth has had a positive impact on FDI inflows in some Asian countries. The studies of Kasibhatla and Sawhney (1996) and Rodrik (1999) for United States reveal unidirectional causal relationship from economic growth to foreign direct investment. Further, Chakraborty and Basu (2002) for India had employed vector error correction model (VECM) to find the short run dynamics of FDI and growth for the years 1974-1996. The empirical result reveals that the causality runs more from real GDP to FDI flows.

Besides, Tsai (1994) employed a simultaneous system of equations to test two-way linkages between FDI and economic growth for 62 countries in the period 1975-1978, and for 51 countries in the period 1983-1986. He found that two-way linkages existed between FDI and growth in the 1980s. Bende-Nabende et al. (2001) also investigated the impact of FDI on economic growth of the ASEAN-5 economies over the period 1970-1996 and found that there exists bi-directional relationship between the two variables. Similarly, Liu et al.

(2002) for China, Basu et al. (2003) for 23 developing countries, Saha (2005) 20 for Latin America and the Caribbean countries, Hansen and Rand (2006) for 31 developing countries, Nguyen Phi Lan (2006) for Vietnam and Mahmoud Al-Iriani et al. (2007) for 6 Gulf Cooperation Countries (GCC) found the bi-directional causality between foreign direct investment and gross domestic product.

On the other side, Alam (2000) in his comparative study of FDI and economic growth for Indian and Bangladesh economy stressed that though the impact of FDI on growth is more in case of Indian economy, yet it is not satisfactory. The study of Pradhan (2002) for India estimated a Cobb-Douglas production function with FDI stocks as additional input variable for the years 1969-1997 and found that the FDI stocks have no significant impact for the whole sample period. Similarly, the other studies such as Bhat et al. (2004) for India, Akinlo (2004) and Ayanwale (2007) for Nigeria, Habiyaremye and Ziesemer (2006) for SSA countries and Jarita Duasa (2007) for Malaysia found no evidence of causal relationship between foreign direct investment and economic growth.

The literature reviewed above pertaining to the causal nexus between foreign direct investment and economic growth in emerging economies is well established. However, the results appear to be ambiguous. Most of the studies employed cointegration test and VECM to examine the causal relationship between FDI and economic growth. It revealed that Johansen's cointegration test and VEC model are the superior techniques to investigate the issue. Johansen's cointegration test examines the presence of (cointegrating) long-run relationship between economic variables in the model. A principal feature of co–integrated variables was that their time paths were influenced by the extent of any deviation from the long–run equilibrium (Walter Enders, 1995).

Thus, vector error correction model that incorporates error correction term represents the percent of correction to any deviation in long–run equilibrium in a single period and also represents how fast the deviations in the long-run equilibrium are corrected. Besides, the VECM provide inferences about the direction of causation between the variables.

Thus, the study can be done by employing Johansen's cointegration test and VEC model to investigate the causality between foreign direct investment and economic growth in the SAARC (South Asian Association for Regional Cooperation) countries.

Understanding causal relations between FDI and economic growth should help policy makers of SAARC countries to plan their FDI policies in a way that enhances growth and development of their economies. The article is divided into different sections providing an overview of FDI inflows in SAARC countries; describing the methodology and data used for empirical analysis; empirical results and discussion of the study and the concluding remarks.

An Overview of FDI Inflows in SAARC Countries

During the past two decades, foreign direct investment (FDI) has become increasingly important in the developing world, with a growing number of developing countries succeeding in attracting substantial and rising amounts of inward FDI. Like other developing world nations, the FDI inflows in SAARC nations started picking up in the mid-1990s as a result of progressive market-oriented reforms, trade liberalisation and investment promotional policies. Table 5.1 presents the FDI inflows into SAARC nations by host country. The table reveals that India followed by Pakistan and Bangladesh are found to attract larger foreign direct investment among the member countries. The table shows the rising trend of absolute FDI inflows in case of Sri Lanka. Flows to Maldives were seemed to be relatively stable since the mid-1990s.

However, FDI flows into Nepal and Afghanistan have been volatile. For Bhutan, the FDI inflows relented significantly in the mid-1990s and early 2000s but rebounded and picked up in the following years.

**Table 5.1: FDI Inflows into SAARC Countries by
Host Country (in US$ million)**

Year	Afghanistan	Bangladesh	Bhutan	India
1990	NA	3.23	1.6	236.6
1996	0.69	231.6	1.4	2525
1997	-1.46	575.2	-0.7	3619
1998	-0.01	576.4	NA	2633
1999	6.04	309.1	1.04	2168
2000	0.17	578.7	0.0002	3585
2001	0.68	354.5	0.0002	5472
2002	0.54	328.3	2.08	5627
2003	2.01	350.2	2.53	4323
2004	0.62	460.4	3.46	5771
2005	3.61	692	9	6676
2006	2.08	625	6.1	16881
2007	2.88	666	78	22950

Contd...

Year	Maldives	Nepal	Pakistan	Sri Lanka
1990	5.6	5.94	278.3	43.3
1996	9.31	19.16	439.3	133
1997	11.4	23.06	711	433
1998	11.5	12.02	506	150
1999	12.3	4.35	532	201
2000	13	-0.48	309	172.9
2001	11.7	20.8	383	171.7
2002	12.4	-5.95	823	196.5
2003	13.5	14.7	534	228.7
2004	14.6	-0.41	1118	233
2005	9.49	2.44	2201	272
2006	13.8	-6.55	4273	480
2007	15.0	6	5333	528.6

Source: UNCTAD FDI/TNC database. NA-denotes not available.

The increasing FDI flows into SAARC nations are mainly due to their liberalised approach to foreign direct investment and changes in foreign direct investment policy after 1990s, such as removal of the requirement of government approval of foreign investment, permission of foreign equity participation of up to 100 percent, permission to negotiate the terms and conditions of payment of royalty and technical fees suited to foreign investors for transferring technology, liberalisation of foreign exchange regime and permission of remittances of principal and dividends from foreign direct investment including an extensive set of fiscal incentives and allowances to foreign investors. Besides, the objectives and policy initiatives of SAARC countries related to economic, trade, financial and monetary areas of regional economic integration with growing number of bilateral treaties for the avoidance of double taxation and multilateral investment agreements that have so far been made by member countries contributed to larger FDI inflows into the region.

Table 5.2 presents the FDI inflows as a percentage of GDP in SAARC member economies. It shows that FDI as a percentage of GDP in SAARC economies seem to be relatively lower, and especially in the case of Afghanistan and Nepal, it remained less than one percent in 1990s and 2000. Similarly, the FDI openness to GDP in Bhutan seems to be less than one percent until 2004, but rose to a peak level of 6.21 percent in 2007.

Besides, FDI as a percentage of GDP for Bangladesh has been relatively stable, and in case of India, Pakistan and Sri Lanka, it shows a growing trend from mid-1990s, largely as a result of progressive liberalisation of FDI policies in most of the sectors in the region as well as the adoption of generally outward looking policies in these nations. Broadly speaking, the trend of foreign direct investment inflows in both absolute and relative terms in SAARC economies does not reveal any clear discernible pattern involving GDP and FDI. It is far from being conclusive in drawing any causal relationship. Thus, a formal econometric analysis is required to empirically examine the FDI-GDP relationships for the sample countries.

Table 52: FDI Inflows as a Percentage of GDP in SAARC Countries

Year	Afghanistan	Bangladesh	Bhutan	India
1991	-0.008	0.004	0.252	0.025
1995	-0.002	0.223	0.016	0.580
2001	0.030	0.724	0.00	1.131
2002	0.011	0.632	0.385	1.116
2003	0.042	0.611	0.402	0.729
2004	0.010	0.743	0.487	0.837
2005	0.052	1.069	1.075	0.825
2006	0.026	0.916	0.661	1.868
2007	0.029	0.856	6.219	2.018

Contd...

Year	Maldives	Nepal	Pakistan	Sri Lanka
1991	2.659	0.068	0.439	0.725
1995	1.812	0.00	0.604	0.486
2001	1.872	0.379	0.532	1.070
2002	1.935	-0.109	1.008	1.165
2003	1.949	0.246	0.546	1.229
2004	1.892	-0.006	0.989	1.144
2005	1.264	0.032	1.698	1.135
2006	1.529	-0.081	2.909	1.753
2007	1.438	0.060	3.187	1.736

Source: Authors' own compilation

Methodology

Johansen's (1988) cointegration and vector error correction model (VECM) was employed to examine the causal nexus between foreign direct investment and economic growth in SAARC countries for the years 1970-2007. Before implementing the cointegration and vector error correction model, econometric methodology needs to verify the stationarity of each individual time series since most macro economic data is non-stationary, i.e., they tend to exhibit a deterministic and/or stochastic trend. Though the cointegration approach applies to non-stationary series, it requires that all variables in the system are integrated of the same order I (1). The first step in the analysis is to test for non-stationarity of the data series.

Variables that are non-stationary can be made stationary by differencing; the number of differencing (d) required to make the series stationary identifies the order of integration I (d). For the purpose, Augmented Dickey-Fuller (1979) and Phillips-Perron (1988) tests were employed to verify the stationarity of the data series and to determine the order of integration of each of the data series studied. If the selected data series are found to be integrated in an identical order, Johansen's cointegration test is employed to examine long-run (cointegrating) relationship among the selected variables.

Once we identify a single cointegration vector among the selected variables, the vector error correction model (VECM) can be employed to establish the Granger causal direction. VECM allows the modeling of both the short-run and long-run dynamics for the variables involved in the model. Engle and Granger (1987) show that cointegration is implied by the existence of a corresponding error correction representation which implies that changes in the dependent variable are a function of the level of the disequilibrium in the cointegrating relationships (captured by error correction term) and changes in other independent variables. According to Granger representation theorem, if variables are cointegrated, then their relationships can be expressed as VECM. Provided that variables in our case are cointegrated, the VECM can be written as:

$$\Delta lnFDI_t = c_1 + \Sigma_{k=1}^{n} \alpha_{1i} \Delta lnFDI_{t-k} + \Sigma_{k=1}^{n} \beta_{2i} \Delta lnGDP_{t-k} + \rho_1 ECT_{t-k} + \varepsilon fdit$$

$$...(1)$$

$$\Delta lnGDP_t = c_2 + \Sigma \beta_{1i} \Delta lnGDP_{t-k} + \Sigma \alpha_{2i} \Delta lnFDI_{t-k} + \rho_2 ECT_{t-k} + \varepsilon gdpit$$
$$\underset{k=1}{\overset{n}{}} \qquad \underset{k=1}{\overset{n}{}}$$

$$...(2)$$

where, Δ is the first difference operator and εfdit and εgdpit are white noise disturbance terms. FDI_t and GDP_t are foreign direct investment and gross domestic product of individual SAARC economies at time 't' respectively and ECT_{t-k} is the lagged error correction term.

In terms of the vector error correction model (VECM) of equation (1) and (2), GDP_t Granger causes FDI_t, if some of the β_{2i} coefficients, i = 1,2,3,......n-1 are not equal to zero and the error coefficient ρ_1 in the equation of FDI flows is significant at convention levels. Similarly, FDI_t Granger causes GDP_t, if some of the α_{2i} coefficients, i = 1,2,3,......n-1 are not zero and the error coefficient ρ_2 in the equation of GDP is significant at convention levels. These hypotheses can be tested by using either t-tests or f-tests on the joint significance of the lagged estimated coefficients. If both FDI_t and GDP_t Granger causes each other, then there is a feedback relationship between foreign direct investment and gross domestic product. The error correction coefficients, ρ_1 and ρ_2 serve two purposes. They are: (i) to identify the direction of causality between foreign direct investment and gross domestic product, and (ii) to measure the speed with which deviations from the long-run relationship are corrected by changes in the foreign direct investment and gross domestic product.

On the other hand, if FDI and GDP are not cointegrated, the standard Granger (1969) bivariate causality is performed without including error correction term. One variable GDP is said to Granger cause another variable, FDI, if GDP can be explained by using past values of FDI. The superiority of the explanation is then investigated if additional lagged values of GDP improve the explanation of FDI. Estimating the following equations performs the standard Granger causality test:

$$\Delta lnFDI_t = c_1 + \Sigma\alpha_{1i}\Delta lnFDI_{t-k} + \overset{n}{\underset{k=1}{\Sigma}} \beta_{2i}\Delta lnGDP_{t-k} + u_{1t} \quad ...(3)$$

$$\Delta lnGDP_t = c_2 + \overset{n}{\underset{k=1}{\Sigma}} \beta_{1i}\Delta lnGDP_{t-k} + \overset{n}{\underset{k=1}{\Sigma}} \alpha_{2i}\Delta lnFDI_{t-k} + u_{2t} \quad ...(4)$$

Testing causal directions among the variables of interest, in the Granger sense, causality can be found by testing the null hypothesis Ho: $\beta_{2i} = \alpha_{2i} = 0$. The null hypothesis is accepted or rejected based on the standard Wald f-test to determine the joint significance of the restrictions under the null hypothesis. There is bi-directional causality if both β_{2i} and α_{2i} are significant. GDP Granger causes FDI if β_{2i} is statistically significant but α_{2i} is not; and FDI Granger causes GDP if α_{2i} is statistically significant but β_{2i} is not. This is called unidirectional causality. Hence, from the above equations (3) and (4) it is clear that GDP Granger causes FDI if $\beta_{2i}>0$ and FDI Granger causes GDP if $\alpha_{2i}>0$. If FDI and GDP do not cause each other, all the coefficients of GDP in equation (3) and of FDI in equation (4) should be statistically insignificant.

Finally, the impulse response function (IRF) has been employed to investigate the time paths of log of foreign direct investment (LFDI) in response to one-unit shock to the log of gross domestic product (LGDP) and vice versa. The impulse response function analysis is a practical way to visualize the behaviour of a time series in response to various shocks in the system (Walter Enders, 1995). The plot of the IRF shows the effect of a one standard deviation shock to one of the innovations on current and future values of the endogenous variables. This study includes two variables, FDI and GDP of the individual SAARC economies for the impulse response function technique. Plotting the impulse response function can trace the effects of shocks to εfdit or εgdpt on the time paths of the GDPt or FDIt sequences.

The data used for the study consist of net foreign direct investment inflows and gross domestic product from the

SAARC countries which includes Bangladesh, India, Maldives, Nepal, Pakistan and Sri Lanka. The rest of the SAARC countries, viz. Afghanistan and Bhutan were not considered for the study because of lack of availability of data on foreign direct investment inflows. The data on foreign direct investment inflows are limited and time series of most countries start in the late 1960s and early 1970s, which prevents the consideration of longer time span for the analysis. Hence, the annual time-series data on net foreign direct investment inflows and gross domestic product for Bangladesh, India, Maldives, Nepal, Pakistan and Sri Lanka were considered for the years 1970-2007. The inward foreign direct investment series were compiled from United Nations Commission for Trade and Development (UNCTAD) reports. The real gross domestic product (GDP) series were obtained from International Monetary Fund's International Financial Statistics (IFS) database. The values of both series are expressed in terms of millions of US dollars at current prices.

Empirical Results and Discussions

The unit root property of the data series is crucial for the cointegration and causality analyses. The standard augmented Dickey-Fuller (ADF) and Phillips-Perron (PP) tests were employed to examine stationary property of the selected data series. Table 5.3 depicts the results of Augmented Dickey-Fuller and Phillips-Perron tests for the GDP and FDI series of the SAARC countries. Both the unit root test results reveal that the null hypothesis of unit root for the selected variables such as foreign direct investment and gross domestic product in case of each individual country was not rejected at levels. But, when the series are first differenced, both the series are found to be stationary and integrated at the order of one I (1).

Proven that both the series are integrated of same order I (1), the Johansen cointegration test was performed to examine the presence of long-run relationship between foreign direct investment and gross domestic product for the individual

SAARC countries and the results are presented in Table 5.4. In the table, the Johansen's maximum eigen and trace statistics for each individual SAARC nations namely, Bangladesh, India, Maldives, Nepal, Pakistan and Sri Lanka indicates that the null hypothesis of no cointegrating vector ($r = 0$) can be rejected at five percent significance level, and the alternative hypothesis of at most one cointegrating vector ($r \geq 1$) can be accepted.

Table 5.3: Results of Augmented Dickey-Fuller and Phillip-Perron Unit Root Tests

Country	Variables	Augmented Dickey-Fuller Test Statistics		Phillips-Perron Test Statistics	
		Level			
		Trend	No Trend	Trend	No Trend
Bangladesh	FDI	-0.46	0.48	-1.45	-0.17
	GDP	-1.92	1.16	-2.20	0.78
India	FDI	-0.63	1.22	0.03	1.25
	GDP	0.14	1.46	-0.008	0.99
Maldives	FDI	-2.10	0.48	-1.63	-1.30
	GDP	-0.41	0.45	-0.43	1.53
Nepal	FDI	-1.53	-1.60	-1.52	-1.67
	GDP	-0.02	1.31	0.07	1.05
Pakistan	FDI	-2.12	0.51	-2.41	-0.49
	GDP	0.12	1.35	0.06	1.30
Sri Lanka	FDI	-2.43	-0.26	-2.52	-0.26
	GDP	0.20	0.99	0.35	0.97
First Difference					
Bangladesh	FDI	-6.27*	-6.18*	-6.20*	-6.14*
	GDP	-3.98*	-2.48**	-4.02*	-2.35**
India	FDI	-5.06*	-5.85*	-8.99*	-5.99*
	GDP	-3.83*	-2.01**	-3.93*	-1.98**
Maldives	FDI	-7.42*	6.04*	-8.38*	-7.63*
	GDP	-5.02*	-3.69*	-4.94*	-3.66*
Nepal	FDI	-3.48**	-3.75*	-3.60**	-3.93*
	GDP	-6.70*	-3.73*	-6.81*	-4.07*
Pakistan	FDI	-3.49**	-3.36*	-9.27*	-8.32*
	GDP	-5.21*	-5.25*	-5.18*	-4.67*
Sri Lanka	FDI	-4.42*	-7.12*	-7.66*	-7.81*
	GDP	-4.40*	-2.56**	-6.81*	-4.84*

Notes: * (**)–indicates significance at the one and five percent level respectively. Optimal lag length is determined by the Schwarz Information Criterion (SC) and Newey-West Criterion for the Augmented Dickey-Fuller Test and Phillips-Perron Test respectively.

Therefore, the results support the hypothesis of cointegration between foreign direct investment and gross domestic product, implying that there are stable long-run relationships between the two variables in case of each SAARC countries.

Table 5.4: Results of Johansen's Cointegration Test

Country	vector (r)	Trace Statistics	5 percent Critical Value for Trace Statistics	Max-Eigen Statistics	5 percent Critical Value for Max-Eigen Statistics
Bangladesh	H_0: r = 0	39.66**	19.96	31.49**	15.67
	H_1: r ≥ 1	8.174	9.24	8.174	9.24
India	H_0: r = 0	29.94**	25.32	26.39**	18.96
	H_1: r ≥ 1	3.550	12.25	3.550	12.25
Maldives	H_0: r = 0	34.39**	25.32	23.06**	18.96
	H_1: r ≥ 1	11.33	12.25	11.33	12.25
Nepal	H_0: r = 0	19.47**	15.41	16.70**	14.07
	H_1: r ≥ 1	2.771	3.76	2.771	3.76
Pakistan	H_0: r = 0	21.10**	19.96	20.12**	15.67
	H_1: r ≥ 1	0.986	9.24	0.986	9.24
Sri Lanka	H_0: r = 0	20.54**	19.96	16.55**	15.67
	H_1: r ≥ 1	3.991	9.24	3.991	9.24

Notes: **–indicates significance at five percent level. The significant of the statistics is based on 5 percent critical values obtained from Osterwald-Lenum (1992). r is the number of cointegrating vectors. H_0 represents the null hypothesis of presence of no cointegrating vector and H_1 represents the alternative hypothesis of presence of cointegrating vector.

After confirming the existence of single cointegrating vector among foreign direct investment and gross domestic product for the SAARC economies namely, Bangladesh, India, Maldives, Nepal, Pakistan and Sri Lanka, we should search for proper vector error correction model (VECM) to determine the direction of long-run causation. By using the definition of cointegration, the Granger Representation Theorem (Engle and Granger, 1987), which states that if a set of variables are cointegrated, then there exists a valid error correction representation of the data. For the purpose, the VECM is estimated and it is presented in Table 5.5. Besides, the vector error correction model is sensitive to the selection of optimal lag length and the necessary lag length of foreign direct investment and gross domestic product series is determined by the Schwarz Information Criterion (SC) and it reveals optimal lag of one and two for India, Maldives, Pakistan and Sri Lanka and Bangladesh and Nepal respectively. In Table 5.5, the VECM result for Bangladesh shows that the error correction coefficient, ECT_{t-1}, (-0.733) in FDI equation is negative and statistically significant at one percent level, implying that the direction of causality runs interactively through error-correction term from the GDP to FDI.

Table 5.5 Results of Vector Error Correction Model Pertaining to Causal Nexus between FDI and GDP in SAARC Countries

Name of the Country	Regression Equation	C	ΔFDI_{t-1}	ΔFDI_{t-2}	ΔGDP_{t-1}
Bangladesh	ΔFDI on ΔGDP	-0.045 (-0.21)	-0.416 (-1.81)	-0.080 (-0.49)	0.077 (0.350)
	ΔGDP on ΔFDI	0.0001 (0.01)	-0.034 (-2.89)*	-0.015 (-1.75)	-0.006 (-0.58)
India	ΔFDI on ΔGDP	0.029 (0.16)	0.271 (1.62)	-	0.170 (0.06)
	ΔGDP on ΔFDI	0.004 (0.38)	-0.007 (-0.64)	-	-0.446 (-2.60)*
Maldives	ΔFDI on ΔGDP	0.0007 (0.005)	0.157 (0.90)	-	0.002 (0.002)
	ΔGDP on ΔFDI	0.001 (0.04)	-0.086 (-2.79)*	-	-0.203 (-1.22)
Nepal	ΔFDI on ΔGDP	-0.097 (-0.48)	0.449 (1.48)	0.308 (1.990)**	-1.538 (-0.68)
	ΔGDP on ΔFDI	0.004 (0.34)	0.049 (2.38)**	0.017 (1.58)	-0.741 (-4.82)*
Pakistan	ΔFDI on ΔGDP	-0.189 (-0.94)	-0.199 (-1.10)	-	1.053 (0.56)
	ΔGDP on ΔFDI	0.026 (2.29)**	-0.040 (-3.87)	-	0.274 (2.53)**
Sri Lanka	ΔFDI on ΔGDP	-0.091 (-0.33)	0.184 (1.07)	-	5.393 (2.44)**
	ΔGDP on ΔFDI	0.002 (0.15)	-0.023 (-2.01)**	-	-0.259 (-1.70)

Contd...

Name of the Country	ΔGDP_{t-2}	ECT_{t-1}	F-Statistic	Inference
Bangladesh	0.139 (0.880)	-0.733 (-2.77)*	21.33	FDI↔GDP
	-0.008 (-1.05)	0.034 (2.52)**	12.85	
India	-	-1.497 (-5.78)*	28.67	GDP→FDI
	-	0.007 (0.421)	12.70	
Maldives	-	-1.826 (-5.92)*	51.18	FDI↔GDP
	-	0.200 (3.63)*	17.46	
Nepal	0.645 (0.290)	-2.032 (-4.96)*	27.18	FDI↔GDP
	-0.486 (-3.21)*	-0.059 (-2.12)**	16.67	
Pakistan	-	-0.420 (-1.98)**	13.44	FDI↔GDP
	-	0.120 (9.80)*	49.30	
Sri Lanka	-	-1.668 (-6.41)*	31.93	FDI↔GDP
	-	-0.006 (-0.34)	11.67	

Notes: Optimal lag length is determined by the Schwarz Information Criterion (SC): FDI and GDP are the Foreign Direct Investment and Gross Domestic Product respectively, * and ** denote the significance at the one and five percent level, respectively. Parenthesis shows t-statistics, * (**)–indicates significance at one and five percent level, respectively.

Moreover, the estimate of ECT_{t-1} suggests the validity of long-run equilibrium relationship among the variables. It also implies that 73 percent of disequilibrium from the pervious period's shock converges back to the long-run equilibrium in the current period. Besides, the coefficients of FDI_{t-1} and ECT_{t-1} in GDP equation are found to be statistically significant at one and five percent level respectively, signifying that direction of causality also run from FDI to GDP in case of Bangladesh. Hence, there exists a long-run causal between FDI and GDP runs in both directions for Bangladesh. Similarly, the VECM result for Maldives, Nepal, Pakistan and Sri Lanka exhibits long-run relation between FDI and GDP and bidirectional causal linkage exists between FDI and GDP. For India, the result of VECM shows that error correction coefficient, ECT_{t-1}, in FDI equation is found to have expected negative sign and significant at one percent level, implying that the direction of causality runs interactively through error-correction term from the GDP to FDI. This indicates a one-way long-run causality runs from GDP to FDI for India.

Finally, the impulse response functions were applied to reveal the dynamic causal relationships between FDI and economic growth in SAARC nations. These illustrate the response of GDP to the innovation in FDI and by GDP itself and also show the response of FDI to the innovation in GDP and by FDI itself.

The impulse response function for the Bangladesh reveals the positive response of GDP from a FDI shock throughout the longer time period. Besides, the response of FDI to GDP shock begins with immediate negative effect but has a greater positive impact on FDI inflows for the longer time period. This indicates that there is significant positive impact of FDI on GDP and vice versa.

This result is consistent with the earlier findings of vector error correction model in case of Bangladesh. For India, the FDI shock has created a positive impact on GDP. Besides, the GDP shock has an immediate positive impact on FDI for the longer time period. In the case of Maldives, the response of GDP to a shock in FDI is elevated for the first two years and has stable positive effect on GDP thereafter. Besides, the response of FDI to GDP shock begins with immediate positive effect and has greater positive effect on FDI inflows for the longer time period. For Nepal, FDI shock has a positive effect on GDP.

Similarly, the GDP shock has a positive effect on FDI for the longer time period, reflecting a positive impact of FDI on GDP and vice versa in the long run. Relatively similar results were obtained for Pakistan and Sri Lanka. The findings from impulse response functions for each SAARC countries are consistent with the results of vector error correction model.

Concluding Remarks

Johansen cointegration technique followed by the vector error correction model (VECM) was employed to investigate the causal nexus between foreign direct investment (FDI) and economic growth in SAARC countries. The Johansen cointegration result establishes a long-run relationship between foreign direct investment and gross domestic product (GDP) for the sample of SAARC nations, namely, Bangladesh, India, Maldives, Nepal, Pakistan and Sri Lanka. The empirical results of vector error correction model exhibit a long-run bi-directional causal link between GDP and FDI for the selected SAARC nations except India. The test results show that there is a one-way long-run causal link running from GDP to FDI for India.

The present study suggests that the enhancement of country's economic growth performance was much needed to attract foreign direct investment flows rather than liberalised FDI-oriented policy efforts in the case of India. For rest of the SAARC nations, the economic growth performance is the driving force behind the surge in FDI inflows in addition to being a consequence of these inflows.

Hence, these countries pursue the ongoing economic policies with regard to growth and FDI more vigorously. Predominantly, they should adopt effective policy measures that would substantially enlarge and diversify their economic base, improve local skills and build up a stock of human capital recourses capabilities, enhance economic stability and liberalise their market in order to attract as well as benefit from long-term FDI inflows.

References

Aghion, P. Comin, D. and Howitt, P. (2006), "When does Domestic Saving Matter for Economic Growth?", *NBER Working Paper No.* 12275, National Bureau of Economic Research, Cambridge, Mass.

Akinlo, A. (2004), Foreign Direct Investment and Growth in Nigeria: An Empirical Investigation. Journal of Policy Modeling, 26, No. 5, pp. 627-639.

Alam, M. S. (2000), "FDI and Economic Growth of India and Bangladesh: A comparative study", *Indian Journal of Economics*, Vol. 80 (1), No. 316, pp. 1-15.

Ayanwale, A. B. (2007), "FDI and economic Growth: Evidence from Nigeria", AERC *Research Paper No. 165, African Economic Research Consortium, Nairobi, Kenya.*

Bacha, E. L. (1974), "Foreign capital inflow and the output growth rate of the recipient country", *Journal of Development Studies*, Vol. 10, No. 3-4, pp. 374-381.

Balasubramanyam, V. N., Salisu, M. A. and D. Sapsford (1996), "Foreign Direct Investment and Growth in EP and IS Countries", *Economic Journal*, Vol. 106, No. 434, pp. 92-105.

Basu, P., Chakraborty, C. and D. Reagle (2003), "Liberalization, FDI, and Growth in Developing countries: a Panel Cointegration Approach", *Economic Inquiry*, Vol. 41, No. 3, pp. 510-516.

Bende-Nabende, A., Ford, J. and Slater, J. (2001), "FDI, Regional Economic Integration and Endogenous Growth: Some Evidence from Southeast Asia", *Pacific Economic Review*, Vol. 6, No. 3, pp. 383-399.

Bhat, K. S., Tripura Sundari, C. U. and K. D. Raj (2004), "Causal Nexus between Foreign Direct Investment and Economic Growth in India" *Indian Journal of Economics*, Vol. 85, No. 337, pp. 171-185.

Blomstrom, M. and A. Kokko (1998), "Multinational Corporations and Spillovers", *Journal of Economic Surveys*, Vol. 12, No. 2, pp. 247-277.

Blomstrom, M., Lipsey, R., and Zejan, M. (1992), "What explains developing country growth?", NBER Working Paper No. 4132, National Bureau of Economic Research, Cambridge, Mass.

Borensztein, E., De Gregorio, J., Lee, J. W. (1998), "How does foreign direct investment affect economic growth?", *Journal of International Economics*, Vol. 45, No. 1, pp. 115-135.

Bornschier, V. (1980), "Multinational Corporations and Economic Growth: A Cross National Test of the Decapitalisation Thesis", *Journal of Development Economics*, Vol. 7, No. 2, pp. 115-135.

Campos, N. F. and Kinoshita, Y. (2002), "Foreign Direct Investment as Technology Transferred: Some Panel Evidence from the

Transition Economies", CEPR Discussion Paper No. 3417, Centre for Economic Policy Research, London, United Kingdom.

Carkovic, M. and R. Levine (2002), "Does Foreign Direct Investment Accelerate Economic Growth?", Working Paper No. 2, Department of Business Finance, University of Minnesota.

Chakraborty, C. and P. Basu (2002), "Foreign Direct Investment and Growth in India: A Cointegration Approach", *Applied Economics*, Vol. 34, No. 9, pp. 1061-1073.

De Mello Jr. and Luiz, R. (1999), "Foreign Direct Investment in developing Countries and Growth: A Selective Survey", *The Journal of Development Studies*, Vol. 34, No. 1, pp. 1-34.

Dickey, D. A. and Fuller, W. A. (1979), "Distribution of the Estimations for Autoregressive Time Series with a Unit Root", *Journal of the American Statistical Association*, Vol. 47, pp. 427-431.

Jarita Duasa (2007), "Malaysian Foreign Direct Investment and Growth: Does Stability Matter?", *Journal of Economic Cooperation among Islamic Countries* , Vol. 28, No. 2, pp. 83-98.

Engle, R. F. and Granger C. W. J. (1987), "Co-integration and Error Correction Representation, Estimation and Testing", *Econometrica*, Vol. 55, No. 5, pp. 286-301.

Eric Fosu O-A and Joseph Magnus, F. (2006), "Bounds Testing Approach to Cointegraton: An Examination of Foreign Direct Investment Trade and Growth Relationships", *American Journal of Applied Sciences*, Vol. 3, No. 11, pp. 2079-2085.

Feridun, Mete and Sissoko, Yaya (2006), "Impact of FDI on Economic Development: A Causality Analysis for Singapore, 1976-2002", Paper Presented in 6th Global Conference on Business and Economics at Harvard University, USA.

Granger, C. (1969), "Investigating causal relationship by econometric models and cross spectral methods", *Econometrica*, Vol. 37, No. 3, pp. 424-458.

Griffin, K. B. (1970), "Foreign Capital, Domestic Savings and Development", *Oxford Bulletin of Economics and Statistics*, Vol. 32, No. 2, pp. 99-112.

Habiyaremye, A. and T. Ziesemer (2006), "Absorptive Capacity and export diversification in SSA countries," UNU-UNU MERIT Working Paper Series No. 2006-030, United Nations University.

Haddad, M. and Harrison, A. (1993), "Are there spillovers from direct foreign investment?", *Journal of Development Economics*, Vol. 42, No.1, pp. 51-74.

Hansen, H. and *Rand, J. (2006),* "On the causal links between *FDI* and growth in *developing countries"*, *World Economy* Vol. 29, No. 1, pp. 21-41.

Har Wai Mun, Teo Kai Lin and Yee Kar Mun (2008), "FDI and economic growth relationship: An empirical study on Malaysia", *International Business Research*, Vol. 1, No. 2, pp. 11-18.

Jackson, S. and Markowski, S. (1995), "The Attractiveness of countries to Foreign Direct Investment: Implications for the Asia-Pacific region", *Journal of Trade*, Vol. 29, No. 5, pp. 159-179.

Johansen, S. (1988), "Statistical Analysis and Cointegrating Vectors", *Journal of Economic Dynamics and Control*, Vol. 12, No. 2-3, pp. 231-254.

Kashibhatla, K. and B. Sawhney (1996), "FDI and Economic Growth in the US; Evidence from cointegration and Granger Causality Test", *Rivista Internazioriale di Sceinze Economiche e Commerciali*, Vol. 43, pp. 411-420.

Lensink, R. and Morrissey, O. (2006), "Foreign Direct Investment: Flows, Volatility, and the Impact on Growth", *Review of International Economics*, Vol. 14, No. 3, pp. 478-493.

Liu, X., Burridge, P., Sinclairs, P. J. N. (2002), "Relationships between Economic Growth, Foreign Direct Investment and Trade: Evidence from China", *Applied Economics*, Vol. 34, No. 11, pp. 1433-1440.

Lucas, L. (1990), "Why Doesn't Capital Flow from Rich to Poor Countries", *AEA Papers and Proceedings*, Vol. 80, No. 2, pp. 92-96.

Lucas, R. (1988), "On the Mechanics of Economic Development", *Journal of Monetary Economics*, Vol. 22, No. 1, pp. 3-42.

Lumbila, K. (2005), "What Makes FDI Work? A Panel Analysis of the Growth Effect of FDI in Africa", Africa Region Working Paper Series No.80, Africa Region, The World Bank.

Mahmoud Al-Iriani and Fatima Al-Shamsi (2007), "Foreign Direct Investment and Economic Growth in the GCC Countries: An Empirical Investigation Using Heterogeneous Panel Analysis", Working Paper, United Arab Emirates University.

Mankiw, N., Romer, D. and Weil, D. (1992), "A Contribution to the

Empirics of Economic Growth", *The Quarterly Journal of Economics*, Vol. 107, No. 2, pp. 408-437.

Mansfield, E. and Romeo, A. (1980), "Technology Transfer to Overseas Subsidiaries by U.S.-based Firms", *Quarterly Journal of Economics*, Vol. 95, No. 4, pp. 737-750.

Marwah, K. and Tavakoli, A. (2004), "The Effect of Foreign Capital and Imports on Economic Growth: Further Evidence from Four Asian Countries (1970-1998)", *Journal of Asian Economics*, Vol. 15, No. 2, pp. 399-413.

Mencinger, J. (2003), "Does Foreign Direct Investment Always Enhance Economic Growth?", *Kyklos*, Vol. 56, No. 4, pp. 491-509.

Nguyen Phi Lan (2006), Foreign Direct Investment in Vietnam: Impact on Economic Growth and Domestic Investment, mimeo, Centre for Regulation and Market Analysis, University of South Australia.

O'Hearn, D. (1990), "TNCs, intervening mechanisms and economic growth in Ireland: A longitudinal test and extension of Bomschier model", *World Development*, Vol. 18, No. 1, pp. 417-429.

Osterwald-Lenum, M. (1992), "A Note with Quantiles of the Asymptotic Distribution of the Maximum Likelihood Cointegration Rank Test Statistic", *Oxford Bulletin of Economics and Statistics*, Vol. 54, No. 3, pp. 461-472.

Phillips, P. and Perron, P. (1988), "Testing for a Unit Root in Time Series Regression", *Biometrica*, Vol. 75, No. 2, pp. 335-346.

Pradhan, J. P. (2002), "Foreign Direct Investment and Economic Growth in India: A Production Function Analysis", *Indian Journal of Economics*, Vol. 82, No. 327, pp. 582-586.

Prebisch, R. (1968), "*Development problems of the peripheral countries and the terms of trade*", In: Theberge JD (ed.) Economics of trade and development, Wiley, New York.

Ram, R. and Zhang, K. H. (2002), "Foreign Direct Investment and Economic Growth: Evidence from Cross-Country Data for the 1990s", *Economic Development and Cultural Change*, Vol. 51, No. 1, pp. 205-215.

Ramirez, M. D. (2000), "Foreign Direct Investment in Mexico: A Cointegration Analysis", *The Journal of Development Studies*, Vol. 37, No. 1, pp. 138-162.

Reyadh, Y. F. and Khalifa, H. G. (2009), "Foreign Direct Investment and Economic Growth: The Case of the GCC Countries", *International Research Journal of Finance and Economics*, Issue 29, July, pp. 134-145.

Rodrik, D. (1999), *"The New Global Economy and Developing Countries: Making Openness Work"*, Policy Essay No. 24, Overseas Development Council, Washington, D.C.

Romer, M. (1986), "Increasing Returns and Long-Run Growth", *Journal of Political Economy*, Vol. 94, No. 5, pp. 1002-1037.

Romer, M. (1987), "Growth Based on Increasing Returns Due to Specialization", *American Economic Review*, Vol. 77, No. 1, pp. 56-62.

Romer, P. (1993), "Idea Gaps and Object Gaps in Economic Development", *Journal of Monetary Economics*, Vol. 32, No. 3, pp. 543-573.

Saha, N. (2005), "Three Essays on Foreign Direct Investment and Economic Growth in Developing Countries", Working paper, UTAH State University, Logan, Utah.

Saltz, S. (1992), "The negative correlation between foreign direct investment and economic growth in the Third World: theory and evidence", *Rivista Internazionale di Scienze Economiche e Commerciali*, Vol. 39, pp. 617-633.

Singer, H. (1950), "The Distributions of Gains between Investing and Borrowing Countries", *American Economic Review*, Vol. 40, No. 2, pp. 473-485.

Solow, R. M. (1956), "A Contribution to the Theory of Economic Growth", *Quarterly Journal of Economics*, Vol. 70, No. 1, pp. 65-94.

Stoneman, C. (1975), "Foreign capital and economic growth", *World Development*, Vol. 3, No.1, pp. 11-26.

Tsai, P. (1994), "Determinants of Foreign Direct Investment and Its Impact on Economic Growth", *Journal of Economic Development*, Vol. 19, No. 1, pp. 137-163.

UNCTAD (2000), *"The Competitiveness Challenge: Transnational Corporations and Industrial Restructuring in Developing Countries"*, United Nations, Geneva.

Uttama, N. (2005), "Foreign Direct Investment in ASEAN Countries: An Empirical Investigation", Paper presented at the *7th Annual Conference* of the European Trade Study Group (*ETSG*), University College. Dublin, Ireland, 8-10 September 2005.

Walter Enders (1995), *"Applied Econometric Time Series"*, John

Wiley and Sons, Inc., U.S.A

Weisskof, T. E. (1972), "The Impact of Foreign Capital Inflow on Domestic Savings in Underdeveloped Countries", *Journal of International Economics*, Vol. 2, No. 1, pp. 25-38.

6

Globalisation and the Indian Economy

Amrik Singh Sudan, Rais Ahmad and Radha Gupta

Introduction

The 1990s witnessed a paradigm shift towards market-oriented economic policies and a careful dismantling of obstacles in its wake. This has helped the smaller, emerging economies gain access to world markets, emergent technologies and collaborations. This has also given them a window to the developed world and helped them understand the significant role of globalisation as an instrument, which could be utilised not just to achieve economic efficiency, but also eradicate poverty.

Globalisation has also resulted in the creation of a new business framework. More changes can be expected in the business scenario specifically in terms of openness, adaptiveness and responsiveness. The most important dimensions of economic globalisation are: (a) breaking down of national barriers; (b) international spread of trade, financial and production activities, and (c) growing power of transnational corporations and international financial institutions in these processes. While economic globalisation is a very uneven process, with increased trade and investment being focused in a few countries, almost all countries are greatly affected by this process.

A major feature of globalisation is the growing concentration and monopolisation of economic resources and power by transnational corporations and by global financial firms and funds. This process has been termed transnationalisation, in which fewer and fewer transnational corporations are gaining a large and rapidly increasing proportion of world economic resources, production and market shares. Where a multinational company used to dominate the market of a single product, a big transnational company (TNC) now typically produces or trades in an increasing multitude of products, services and sectors. Through mergers and acquisitions, fewer and fewer of these TNCs now control a larger and larger share of the global market, whether in commodities, manufactures or services.

Another feature of the current globalisation process is the globalisation of national policies and policy-making mechanism. National policies (including economic, social, cultural and technological) that until recently were determined by the States and people within a country have increasingly come under the influence of international agencies and processes or by big private corporations and economic/financial players. This has led to the narrowed ability of governments and people to make choices from options in economic, social and cultural policies.

Most developing countries have seen their independent policy-making mechanism capacity eroded, and have to adopt policies influenced by other entities, which may on balance be detrimental to the countries concerned. The developed countries, where the major economic players reside, and which also control the processes and policies of international economic agencies, are better able to maintain control over their own national policies as well as determine the policies and practices of international institutions and the global system. However, it is also true that the large corporations have taken over a large part of decision-making even in the developed countries, at the expense of the power of the state or political and social leaders.

Benefits of Globalisation to the Indian Economy

Benefits of globalisation are expected to accrue to all the various economies of the world—whether developed or the developing ones—through the channels of trade, capital movements and financial flows. The process of globalisation got a boost after the announcement of Industrial Policy in 1991. The expected benefits of globalisation to the Indian economy are as follows:

1. **Access to New Technology:** For a developing country like India, the process of globalisation has paved the way for import of advanced technology. The domestic companies can acquire new technology through outright purchase of joint ventures and other arrangement.

2. **Reduction in Cost of Production:** Some companies like petroleum and mining often go global to secure a reliable or cheaper source of raw materials. Cheap labour in other countries may also lure foreign investors. In some cases, the whole manufacturing of a product may be carried out in foreign locations and in some cases only certain stages of production may be carried out abroad.

3. **Growth Opportunities in Foreign Markets:** Growth opportunity in foreign markets is a strong attraction for foreign companies. Some countries realize that their domestic markets are no longer adequate and rich to absorb the whole production of goods and services. Japan flooded the US market with automobiles and electronics because the home market was not sufficiently large enough to absorb whatever was produced. Some European Countries have gone global for the same reasons. Moreover, in a number of developing countries, the population and income are growing fast. Asians have become the biggest consumers in the world market, even though market for several goods is not very substantial at present in these countries. Foreign companies are establishing themselves considering the future potential.

4. **Improvement of Competitive Strength:** Globalisation will expose domestic industry in developing countries to foreign competition. They will be under pressure to improve efficiency and quality and reduce costs. Thus,

globalisation will help to improve the competitive strength and economic growth of developing nations.

5. **Satisfaction of Consumers:** Better quality of low priced goods and services will become available to consumers. This, along with a wider choice in consumption will help to improve the standard of living in developing countries. Over a period of time, the proportion of people below the poverty line will go down. Consumers would also get access to products manufactured in any part of the world.

6. **Increased Volume of Trade:** With economic integration of the nations becoming a reality, there has been a phenomenal increase in world trade. Each nation is able to specialise in the production of goods and services in which it has a comparative advantage and trade with other nation. This would lead to better allocation and utilization of the resources of the world economy.

7. **Spin off Benefits:** Globalisation has certain spin off benefits also. It would help the companies to improve their domestic business as well as the image of the country. Foreign exchange earnings enable the companies to import capital goods and technology which could not otherwise have been possible in developing countries.

Challenges of Globalisation

The issue that concerns developing countries is how one can ensure greater participation of the weaker economies in the global process and what needs to be done to ensure that the course of globalisation benefits more people in more countries. The uneven and unequal nature of the present globalisation is manifested in the fast growing gap between the rich and poor people of the world and between developed and developing countries; and by the large differences among nations in the distribution of gains and losses.

This imbalance leads to polarisation between countries and groups that gain, and the many countries and groups in society that lose out or are marginalised. Globalisation, polarisation, wealth concentration and marginalisation are therefore linked through the same process. In this process, investment resources, growth and modern technology are focused on a few countries, mainly in North America, Europe, Japan and a few East Asian countries. A majority of developing countries are excluded from the process, or are participating in it in marginal ways.

Although the developed world is in a dominant position and has been prepared to use this to further their control of the global economy, the developing countries have not done well in organising themselves to co-ordinate on substantial policy and negotiating positions. The developed countries, on the other hand, are well-organised within their own countries, with well-staffed departments dealing with international trade and finance, and with university academics and private and quasi-government think tanks helping to obtain information and map policies and strategies. They also have well-organised associations and lobbies associated with their corporations and financial institutions, which have great influence over the government departments.

On the positive side, globalisation has compelled developing countries to improve overall economic management, and make their economies efficient. To get a share of global capital and technology, developing countries have to upgrade their social and economic institutions through administrative, legislative and legal reforms. The quality of governance has to improve to encourage productivity and efficiency. Political stability has to be established. In this context, following lessons can be drawn from East Asian countries:

1. Developing human capital is a basic pre-requisite. Successful globalisation and the knowledge economy require educated, healthy and skilled people.
2. It is necessary to build up domestic savings and put them to productive use.
3. Sound economic management and macro-economic

balances are necessary. Large fiscal deficit is a serious obstacle to globalisation.

4. Good governance at the national and sub-national levels builds confidence among investors.
5. Transparency has to be established in the functioning of both government and business units.
6. Free and open market economies require effective regulatory authorities because role of government changes from control and regulation to governance and facilitation.
7. Modernised capital markets with effective regulatory authorities are necessary to impart confidence to investors by maintaining stability and regulating speculative forces.

The socio-economically disadvantaged are yet to benefit from globalisation. The challenge to overcome the scourge of poverty remains a daunting task. The support of the poor for reforms and their involvement in the development process can be achieved only if they start benefiting from government policies. It is necessary to ensure that the poor and the deprived have a greater stake in economic reforms than at present, for mobilising their enthusiastic participation in the development process. Economic reforms must be guided by compassion and distributive justice. Improvement in living conditions of the poorest and the weakest sections of society should be high priority areas of welfare and development programmes/schemes of the government.

Adverse Effects of Globalization on Women

With the growing globalization and liberalization of the economy as well as increased privatization of services, women as a whole have been left behind and not been able to partake the fruits of success. Mainstreaming of women into the new and emerging areas of growth is imperative. This will require training and skill upgradation in emerging trades, encouraging more women to take up vocational training and employment in the boom sectors. This will also require women to migrate to cities and metros for work. Provision of safe housing and other gender friendly facilities at work will need to be provided.

Another facet of globalization is related to the fact that many persons, especially women, will be severely affected with the advent of setting up of industrial parks, national highways, special economic zones (SEZs) etc. as huge tracts of farm land are likely to be acquired for this purpose.

This would require massive resettlement of the displaced persons and their families. It is, therefore, essential that a viable resettlement policy and strategy is formulated and put in place immediately which clearly reflects the needs of women impacted by globalization/displacement.

With the removal of all quantitative restrictions on the import of various products, the self-employed women's groups, especially in the informal sector, have started facing competition from the low-priced imported consumer goods which are invading the Indian market.

Although this has the imminent danger of displacing a large number of employed/self-employed women, but at the same time, the process of globalization has also opened up opportunities for women entrepreneurs for exporting their products to the markets all over the world. Globalization has thus opened up new challenges for the realization of the goal of women's empowerment.

Hence, strategies should be designed to enhance the capacity of women and empower them to cope with the negative economic and social impacts of the globalization process.

Several studies have indicated that adverse consequences of globalisation are disproportionately borne by women. Increased mechanization leading to displacement of female unskilled workers, increased migration of male workers in traditionally women-dominated areas, increase in female-headed households due to migration of males, are some of the trends established in various studies.

Globalization has presented new challenges for the realization of the goal of women's equality, the gender impact of which has not been systematically evaluated fully. However, it is evident that there is a need for re-framing policies for access to employment and equality of employment. Benefits of the growing global economy have been unevenly distributed leading to wider economic disparities, the feminization of poverty, increased gender inequality through deteriorating working conditions and unsafe working environment especially in the informal economy and rural areas. Strategies need to be designed to enhance the capacity of women and empower them to meet the negative social and economic impacts, which may flow from the globalization process.

With upgradation of skills, opportunities for employment of women exist in several areas such as health services, food processing and crafts. Key areas of concern include women in small subsistence farming households, women workers in garment and textiles who will face increased competition following the phasing out of the Multi Fibre Agreement in 2005, and women displaced by new technologies in sectors such as construction, which have traditionally absorbed large number of women.

With the onset of trade liberalisation, women in India today are linked to the global economy to a very significant extent, as producers, entrepreneurs, service providers, consumers and citizens. There is a need to identify capacity constraints and entry barriers that prevent women from securing gains from trade. Trade-related awareness and capacity building of the women stakeholders need to be prioritised.

The globalization process has, in some countries, resulted in policy shifts in favour of more open trade and financial flows, privatization of state-owned enterprises and in many cases, lower public spending particularly on social services. This change has transformed patterns of production and accelerated technological advances in information and communication and affected the lives of women, both as workers and consumers. In a large number of countries, particularly in developing and least developed countries, these changes have also adversely impacted the lives of women and have increased inequality. The gender impact of these changes has not been systematically evaluated. Globalization has also affected cultural values, lifestyles and forms of communication.

In countries with economies in transition, women are bearing most of the hardships induced by the economic restructuring and being the first to lose jobs in times of recession. They are being squeezed out from fast growth sectors. Loss of childcare facilities due to elimination or privatization of state work places, increased need for older care without the corresponding facilities, continuing inequality of access to training for finding re-employment and to productive assets for entering or expanding businesses are current challenges facing women in these countries.

Opportunities Offered by Globalization: Science and technology, as fundamental components of development, are transforming patterns of production, contributing to the creation of jobs and new job classifications, and ways of working, and contributing to the establishment of a knowledge-based society. Technological change can bring new opportunities for all women in all fields if they have equal access, and adequate training. Women should also be actively involved in the definition, design, development, implementation and gender impact evaluation of policies related to these changes. Many women world-wide are yet to effectively use these new communication technologies for networking, advocacy, exchange of information, business, education, media consultation and e-commerce initiatives. For instance, millions of the world's poorest women and men still do not have access to and benefits from science and technology and are currently excluded from this new field and the opportunities it presents.

The patterns of migratory flows of labour are changing.

Women and girls are increasingly involved in internal, regional and international labour migration to pursue many occupations mainly in farm labour, domestic work and some forms of entertainment work. While this situation increases their earning opportunities and self-reliance, it also exposes them—particularly the poor, uneducated, unskilled and/or undocumented migrants—to inadequate working conditions, increased health risk, the risk of trafficking, economic and sexual exploitation, racism, racial discrimination and xenophobia, and other forms of abuse.

Further, globalization has dramatically changed the conditions under which the work for gender equality must be carried out, especially in high growth countries like India. While globalization has generated opportunities for local producers and entrepreneurs to reach international markets, it has at times intensified existing inequalities and insecurities for many poor women. Since the gains of globalization are often concentrated in the hands of those with higher education—those who own resources and have access to capital—poor women are usually the least able to seize the long-term opportunities offered.

This disadvantage has been exacerbated as in most of the countries, policies reflect a commitment to global norms of markets and social policy is increasingly determined by market dynamics. Market friendly policies generate high growth rates that fail to translate into improved standards of health, education and human security. Feminist scholars have highlighted the gendered impact of such policies, many of which increase women's job vulnerability, unpaid work burden, while reducing state level resources that might be used to provide a social safety net. Owing to dissent voiced by feminist scholars on the widespread assumption that gender inequality as a challenge can be overcome with effective and sustained advocacy as it is more about mindsets and less about policies, especially economic policies, there have been some attempts to integrate economic and social policies but gender concerns have not been accorded requisite attention. These disadvantages have led to a situation where gains in women's economic opportunities lag behind those in women's capabilities.

To sum up, globalisation is an irreversible trend and developing economies are also inevitably involved in the process. Developed countries should, therefore, carefully consider how to restructure the world trading system to accommodate developing economies, by enabling them to benefit from globalisation while minimising external shocks. The World Trade Organization (WTO) should work more effectively, through an enlargement of waiver clauses which recognises the weaker position of developing countries.

Despite distortions and aberrations, globalisation is a reality. Developments in information and communication technologies are unifying markets and people, cutting across barriers of space and time. At the end of the day, one has to understand and accept that globalisation is the stratagem for the new millennium. Every country, developed and developing, has to accept this and formulate their economies around it.

7

Global Financial Crisis and the Indian Economy

Anli Suresh

Introduction

The financial turmoil which surfaced in August 2007 in the US financial system as a result of defaults of sub-prime mortgage loans has blown into an unprecedented financial crisis engulfing international money, credit, equity and foreign exchange markets. It was preceded by an extended phase of buoyant world economy characterized by output expansion, burgeoning world trade, favourable financial and economic conditions, liquidity overhang and low interest rates. Economists termed it as a period of Great Moderation.

The Great Moderation soon turned into Great Dismay when global financial turmoil—simmering since August 2007—began unleashing its full fury in September 2008 with a series of failures of major financial institutions.

Excess liquidity in the system encouraged banks and financial institutions, particularly in the US, to lend to sub-prime borrowers. There was a gradual build-up of toxic debt which was aided by shoddy financial engineering in the form of slicing-dicing and re-bundling of mortgage-backed securities. When the global interest rates started hardening, a large chunk of borrowers began defaulting, setting off a crisis in the money market that subsequently spread to other financial markets.

Though adversely affected by global meltdown, Indian economy has shown considerable absorption capacity and resilience. Soon after the start of the crisis, net portfolio flows to India turned negative as foreign institutional investors (FIIs) rushed to sell equity stakes in a bid to replenish overseas cash balances. This had a knock-on effect on the stock market which nosedived to record levels. Supply and demand imbalance in the foreign exchange market led to depreciation of rupee vis-à-vis other currencies. The current account was affected mainly after September 2008 through slowdown in exports. Despite setbacks, however, the balance-of-payments situation of the country remained comfortable.

India has remained relatively immune from the fallout of the crisis due to several reasons including prudential, supervisory and regulatory framework of the Reserve Bank of India (RBI). Moral suasions on the part of Government of India, RBI and Securities and Exchange Board of India (SEBI) have also worked. More importantly, the Indian banking system has shown remarkable market discipline, docility, and sincerity of purpose as against the financial gimmicks and dubious practices (repacking of loans, ninja loans etc.) of the financial institutions in the US. It is heartening to note that in India, complex structures like synthetic securitisations have not been permitted so far.

The Indian approach has focused on gradual, phased and calibrated opening of the domestic financial and external sectors, taking into cognizance reforms in the other sectors of the economy. Financial markets are contributing to efficient channelling of domestic savings into productive uses and—by financing the overwhelming part of domestic investment—are supporting domestic growth. These characteristics of India's external and financial sector management coupled with ample forex reserves reduce the susceptibility of the Indian economy to global turbulence.

Most of the crises over the past few decades have had their roots in developing and emerging countries, often resulting from abrupt reversals in capital flows, and from loose domestic monetary and fiscal policies. In contrast, the current ongoing global financial crisis has had its roots in the US.

Due to increasing globalisation, the contagion of the crisis traversed to the EMEs, including India. Despite the fact that the impact on EMEs been relatively muted, there appears to be some element of ambiguity about the policy lessons for them. Moreover, recent developments have provided an opportunity to EMEs to influence the reform of the international financial architecture. Thus, it is important for EMEs to examine the specific changes they should push forward. The regulatory and supervisory issues known during the recent crisis provides a sound background to emerging market and developing economies, which are still in the process of achieving a more sophisticated, and advanced financial system. Thus, it is important that learning about financial sector regulation and supervision during the recent crisis should guide the EMEs while designing their financial regulatory systems.

In addition, a number of issues need to review in the context of EMEs although they were not the source of the recent crisis. Markets and regulators clearly failed to recognize the problems of flawed incentives, information gaps, pro cyclical lending, and risk concentrations behind the financial innovation boom. This shows the lack of a system-wide approach in regulatory and supervisory mechanisms, particularly across the advanced economies. This limited scope of regulation allowed financial innovations to happen without accompanying risk management practices.

During the recent crisis, central banks in both advanced as well as EMEs resorted to various unconventional policy measures to instil confidence and stabilize the markets. However, uncertainty about the effectiveness of unconventional monetary policy and extraordinary measures might push the boundaries of monetary policy. Furthermore, given the visible pressure on capacity in certain EMEs relative to buoyant domestic demand, as well as rising global commodity and food prices, since the mid-year, risks to inflation in EMEs have increased. Against this background, the following sections highlight the key lessons, which are broadly drawn from the crisis in the context of EMEs, including India.

Review of Literature

According to IMF (2009d), policy responses to global developments have been rapid, wide-ranging, and frequently unorthodox, but were too often piecemeal and failed to arrest the downward spiral. The recent crisis appears to be 'beyond compare' despite the fact that it shares some important features with previous crisis. It had some unique characteristics relating to both its causes and its dynamics (Papademos, 2009). The primary lesson that emerged from the crisis is that financial stability is jeopardized even if there is price stability and macroeconomic stability (Subbarao, 2009d).

Other studies focusing on other past episodes of asset price booms and busts apparently found substantial, albeit unintentional, monetary policy mistakes (Bordo and Jeanne, 2002; Gerdesmeier, et al. 2009; Issing, 2002). Thus, the lesson that re-emerges from the crisis is that monetary policy decisions should be sensitive to the sources of inflation. Papademos (2009), Meltzer (2009) and Orphanides (2010) emphasized that one of the lessons from the recent crisis is that monetary policy tools should also be employed to prevent asset market excesses and the systemic and deflation risks they entail. Bernanke (2010) accorded greater priority to efforts towards strengthening the regulatory system. Mishkin (2008) and Taylor (2010) also did not see any role of monetary policy in bursting asset price bubbles.

Arguing against the role of monetary policy, Mishkin (2008) opined that in most cases, monetary policy should not respond to asset prices per se, but rather to changes in the outlook for inflation and aggregate demand resulting from asset price movements. A report of Squam Lake Working Group on Financial Regulation (June, 2010) emphasized that central banks should be the supervisors of overall financial stability. All the influential reports from major international forums [e.g., the G-20 Working Group I Report (2009), the de Larosière Report (2009), the Turner Review (2009), the Geneva Report (2009), and the Group of Thirty Report (2009)] have highlighted that one factor responsible for the crisis was the gap in the regulatory and supervisory aspects of the financial system. Emphasizing on instituting a macro prudential approach to supervision, IMF (2009a) and Bernanke (2009b) suggest setting up a separate regulator to take care of systemic risk, although Taylor (2010) doubts the efficacy of such proposals. Tarullo (2009) also suggests a major revamp of the regulatory and supervisory system to address the problem of systemic risk.

Andritzky et al. (2009) suggested that two issues require immediate attention, i.e. (i) adapting prudential regulations for explicitly countercyclical tendencies; and (ii) encouraging larger liquidity buffers, perhaps even formal liquid asset minimums, to offset the under-pricing of liquidity risk by financial firms in upturns.

Factors Responsible for the Crisis

The collapse of the US sub-prime mortgage market as the immediate cause of the global financial crisis revealed that some financial products and instruments have become so complex that they posed considerable risk to the global financial system, which, in turn, led the world economy to a crisis in a synchronized mode. However, in order to understand the causes of the crisis, it is important to distinguish between the factors that contributed to rising defaults in the US sub-prime housing loan market and those factors that amplified these losses and resulted in major dislocations in financial markets.

Factors that were directly responsible for rising losses in sub-prime housing can be identified as: (i) the low interest rate/benign macroeconomic environment that encouraged lending and risk taking in a search for higher yield by investing in more complex financial products; (ii) regulatory structures that encouraged the increased use of securitisation and the expansion of the 'originate and distribute' mortgage model; (iii) less attention to credit quality; (iv) lack of due diligence among investors; and (v) weaknesses in risk management systems and regulatory oversight. Other factors that contributed and exacerbated the crisis included: (i) the lack of transparency inherent in complex structured financial products in the over-the counter market (OTC); (ii) difficulties and inexperience in using fair value accounting during periods of stress; (iii) weaknesses in risk management systems across all financial market participants, particularly with regard to liquidity risk; (iv) insufficient disclosure about exposures and risks; (v) high degrees of leverage; and (vi) over-reliance on credit ratings and shortcomings in the credit ratings of structured products.

More broadly, high leverage has been a significant factor amplifying losses, leading to some financial institutions to sell securities in the falling markets as they faced margin calls on earlier price falls. This contributed to downward price spirals (G-20 Study Group, 2008). In short, both macro and micro factors contributed to the financial crisis.

Lessons for Emerging Market Economies Including India

Invalidation of Decoupling Hypothesis: Major EMEs have shown consistently remarkable growth performance in the post-2002 period compared to advanced industrial economies. This led to a new wisdom that emerging markets had become masters of their own destiny and "decoupled" from business cycles in industrial countries. In fact, the EMEs remained largely insulated from the first-round effects of the turbulence at the epicentre of global financial markets. However, as the crisis deepened in advanced economies, the complex and wide-ranging interaction between the financial and the real economy began to have an impact on emerging economies. As the crisis entered the second stage, the impact on the real sector also began to appear. Hence, the decoupling hypothesis proved to be a myth as even countries whose financial sector not or hardly exposed to "toxic assets" affected.

Emerging economies, which had strengthened domestic financial institutions and accumulated massive forex reserves guided by the experience of the financial crises of the 1990s, were not spared. A country like India, notwithstanding its sound banking system and smoothly functioning financial system, also suffered from the spillover effects of the financial crisis through sudden capital flow reversals, as part of the global deleveraging process, and liquidity hiccups, mainly through the confidence channel. Gradually, the real sector was hit by the slowdown in exports, job losses in IT and BPO companies due to lack of demand appetite in the real estate, automobile and consumer durables sectors with a squeeze in credit as the result of a cautious approach by several banks.

When the financial crisis first broke, it perceived that developing countries in general not be affected as: (i) they had undertaken various reform measures to strengthen their domestic banking and financial system in recent years, and (ii) their financial sector was not fully integrated in the global financial system. However, occasional bouts of shock on domestic equity markets became evident due to large capital withdrawals particularly in the post-Lehman scenario. This had implications for disruptions in the respective foreign exchange markets and increasing risk perceptions, causing credit squeezes. However, the second wave coming from the real economy, particularly depressing export demands with related job losses, gradually became a challenge. Although, build-up of forex reserves in the immediate past and the soundness of the domestic financial institutions juxtaposed with massive doses of fiscal stimulus and accommodative monetary policy put the emerging economies on a better footing to face the challenges emanating from global financial crisis, but it was difficult to avoid the contagion effects of the crisis.

The broader lesson of this crisis for EMEs including India is that with increasing globalisation, trade, finance and labour are more strongly integrated in advanced economies than ever before. Consequently, any crisis that affects a major country or group of countries in the global economy or financial system will have implications for EMEs as well, eventually, depending on the nature and magnitude of the crisis. Thus, policymakers need to enhance their capacity to pre-empt the potential of such global shocks while formulating their policies.

Domestic Demand is a More Durable Source of Growth: The impact of the crisis on the external demand of EMEs has been clearly visible since the last quarter of 2008. In the first instance, the downturn in the US, Europe, and subsequently in Japan manifested in a sharp contraction in exports from those emerging market countries that had become the largest exporters to the industrial world. Subsequently, exports declined from other emerging economies whose exports consisted of raw and intermediate goods that shipped to those larger emerging market countries, particularly China, which have become key providers of final manufactured goods in the increasingly complex supply chains.

The growth performance of emerging economies provides evidence that those that were largely dependent on external demand, i.e., exports, for their economic growth were severely affected. The synchronized fall in exports intensified in the first quarter of 2009, with a decline of around 25 percent (y-o-y) in the case of larger EMEs. In some commodity-exporting countries, particularly Chile and Russia, exports fell by more than 40 percent in the first quarter of 2009. Since prices fell sharply as world growth slowed, it led to declining incomes in EMEs, which, in turn, tended to reduce demand and growth. In contrast, in economies where domestic demand dominated as a significant source of GDP, the impact was moderate. Thus, it is reasonable to conclude that a strategy of export-led growth entails greater risks than previously appreciated.

It is not only because global demand is volatile but also because trade appears to be more elastic with respect to the cycle and more vulnerable in downturns. It is clear that domestic demand is a more durable source of growth.

Realizing the adverse impact of the crisis on domestic growth, EMEs may need to review their undue dependency on external demand and attempt to generate domestic demand within their economies. In short, there is a need to re-examine the growth strategies pursued in some major emerging and developing countries. It is now increasingly felt that they should re-orient their growth strategies away from mercantilist trade surpluses towards production for domestic demand and greater expansion of balanced trade among other emerging economies rather than industrial countries.

In the Indian context, a reasonably balanced macroeconomic management appears to have made the country more resilient to external shocks. India did not have excessive current account surplus or deficit; no excessive dependence on exports or external demand; no excessive reliance on investment or consumption expenditure; and, no excessive leverage in most households or corporates or financial intermediaries. Thus, it is worth highlighting that despite the widespread impact of the crisis, India was able to grow by 6.7 percent during 2008-09, 7.4 percent during 2009-10 and 7.7 percent during 2010-11.

Financial Sector Reforms: In emerging market and developing economies, financial development is particularly important for effective mobilisation and deployment of savings. Emerging market economies, still in the process of developing their financial systems, can take this opportunity to learn the correct lessons from the crisis to develop a robust financial sector with a sound systemic oversight framework. The experience of the recent crisis shows that the financial system in most emerging Asian countries was relatively resilient to global shocks as reforms that been put in place after the East Asian crisis fostered transparency and governance and strengthened regulation and supervision.

It led to the development of healthier financial institutions across the region in terms of solvency, liquidity, and profitability. In fact, some argue that a cautious and calibrated approach towards financial sector reforms in most of the emerging Asian economies including India may have turned out to be a blessing in disguise during the recent global crisis. Nonetheless, EMEs need to carry out their own due diligence to ensure that systemic risks are monitored within their countries.

However, the crisis also raised the issue of whether home countries would now be as permissive in encouraging banks' foreign operations given the difficulties of multinational supervision. In other words, it still needs to be seen whether countries would tend to be more protectionists in opening up their financial sectors.

Emphasizing the need to ensure an optimum balance of liberalisation and regulation, Subbarao (2009c) argued, "While liberalisation is important for the growth process, it should be managed to avoid forces of destabilization. One reason of the crisis was the excess liquidity in the system and the resultant search for yield, based on the notion that real value is added through financial engineering. This resulted in build-up of imbalances and excesses in the system, ignored by lax regulation. However, the crisis lessons do not make any case for overregulation as it could suppress growth impulses and conservative policies could prove to be costly".

In India, a judicious approach while formulating financial liberalisation measures turned out to be extremely effective as reflected in the strengthening of public sector banks by recapitalization; preventing some of the financial 'innovations' that allowed risk to be disguised rather than actually reduced; taming the overexposure of domestic banks to what is now seen as toxic assets globally; restraining the excessive bullishness of financial investors in real estate; regulating the activities of systemically important non-bank financial institutions; and speaking out against hasty and potentially risky attempts to liberalize the capital account of the balance of payments.

All these measures stood India in good stead by not only

preventing overenthusiastic responses during the global boom, but also reducing the negative impact of the global slump. Thus, countries should self-insure against future crises by putting in place, as best as they can, robust economic and financial policy frameworks that help minimise their vulnerabilities. However, this does not mean that there should be over-regulation, as this can have significant costs. In short, EMEs need to ensure the right balance between regulation and liberalisation of the financial sector so that their long-term growth prospects do not suffer.

In the context of the Indian financial system, it is important to note that it avoided any major stress because of contagion from the global financial crisis, even though the real economy later exhibited a slowdown in activity in tandem with the trend observed elsewhere. Macro variables such as aggregate credit growth, sectoral credit growth and the incremental credit-deposit ratio of banks have historically been integral components of macro policy framework. Much before the crisis, these variables dovetailed into the prudential regulatory framework for banks. Both, macro prudential and micro-prudential policies adopted by the RBI ensured the financial stability and resilience of the banking system. The timely prudential measures instituted during the high growth period, especially about securitisation, additional risk weights and provisioning for specific sectors, measures to curb dependence on borrowed funds, and leveraging by systemically important NBFCs have stood us in good stead. The reserve requirements through CRR and SLR acted as natural buffers, preventing excessive leverage.

The important difference was that the Indian approach entailed sector-specific prescriptions, unlike others. The relatively low presence of foreign banks also minimized the impact on the domestic economy. Thus, the appropriate regulatory framework in place along with specific prudential measures taken from time to time played an important role in preventing instability in the Indian banking system during the global financial crisis.

Management of Capital Flows: Large capital inflows have been considered a key contributing factor in many financial crises in EMEs in the past. It is clear that whether the crisis originates in emerging economies or advanced economies, capital flows generally reverse from EMEs. In the context of the recent crisis, it noted that in response to the strong capital inflows and abundant liquidity, banks tended to relax their underwriting standards, which gave rise to the formation of asset price bubbles. Although large volatility in capital flows to EMEs has been witnessed since the early 1980s, they are increasingly becoming dependent on the stance of monetary policy in the advanced economies, a factor over which domestic authorities have no control. A sudden drying up of capital flows has followed periods of large capital inflows, well above the financing need. In fact, there is a firm view that during the recent crisis, the 'sudden stops' were largely due to failures and shortcomings in international capital markets rather than lack of a sound policy framework in EMEs. Such large swings in capital flows over a very short period impose significant adjustment costs on EMEs.

The recent crisis once again underscored the potential dangers of large capital inflows in EMEs. At the same time, it is apparent that capital account management and prudent regulation of financial sector go hand in hand. It is evident that EMEs like India which followed a calibrated and well-sequenced approach could minimise the adverse impact of exogenous shocks unlike those (e.g. eastern European economies) which did not use prudential regulatory measures to limit intermediation of foreign inflows through domestic banks and financial institutions. On the issue of management of capital flows, the Bretton Woods Institutions also seem to have drifted somewhat from their earlier approach. The IMF Managing Director, Dominique Strauss-Kahn (2009b), remarked, "a related challenge to exit strategies is managing capital flows to emerging markets...Countries have a number of policy options in their toolkits. In many countries, appreciation should be the key policy response. Other tools include lower interest rates, reserves accumulation, tighter fiscal policy, and financial sector prudential measures. Capital controls can be part of the package of measures. We are completely open-minded. However, we should recognize that all tools have their limitations. Again, we should be pragmatic."

In fact an IMF study by Ostry et al. (2010) argues that capital controls are a "legitimate" tool in some cases for governments facing surges in investment that threaten to destabilize their economies. Recommending the use of both macro and structural policies to steer saving and investment, IMF (2009b) called for re-examining the timing and nature of pre-emptive policy responses to large imbalances and large capital flows. According to the World Bank (2009), "capital restrictions might be unavoidable as a last resort to prevent or mitigate the crisis effects...Capital controls might need to be imposed as a last resort to help mitigate a financial crisis and stabilize macroeconomic developments". Nijathaworn (2009) recommended that, given the risk of formation of asset price bubbles associated with large capital flows, risk management of banks must continue to be strengthened and regulators must be prepared to use macro-prudential measures proactively as necessary to reduce such risk. This means credit standards and bank capital rules must remain vigilant, regardless of the abundance of liquidity.

Emphasizing greater caution in the liberalisation of debt flows, Mohan and Kapur (2010) argue for a calibrated and well-sequenced approach to opening up the capital account and its active management, along with complementary reforms in other sectors. Subramanian and Williamson (2009b) prescribe that institutions like the IMF must recognize that capital inflows can pose serious macroeconomic challenges that may require a different cyclical response. For emerging markets, the policy arsenal against future crises must cover measures to counter cyclically restrict credit growth and leverage, particularly, capital flows.

The recent experience of EMEs with capital flows seems to point towards the potential role for prudential measures to reduce systemic risk associated with large capital inflows, e.g., through constraints on the foreign exchange exposure of domestic institutions and other borrowers. In view of the volatility in capital flows seen recently, it is now widely perceived that the need to introduce a tax on international financial transactions be explored. In fact, eminent persons in finance as the former US Fed Chief, Paul Volcker, and Lord Turner (Chief of the UK Financial Services Authority) suggested such a tax even for domestic financial transactions.

In the Indian context, Reddy (2009) suggested that this idea be examined for the forex market, and also suitably modify the securities transaction tax system and extend it to transactions in participatory notes, though they are traded abroad. Similarly, issues of tax arbitrage and residency be revisited globally. In fact, on October 20, 2009, Brazil announced that it would impose a 2 percent tax on capital flowing into the country to invest in equities and fixed income instruments, while direct investment in the productive economy is not affected. In short, the issue of capital control be revisited and debated as it has emerged as one of the important lessons from the crisis for EMEs.

Thus, it can be concluded that with the prior experience of crisis, emerging Asian and Latin American countries appear to have managed their current accounts and external financing requirements more carefully. In contrast, Central and Eastern Europe, with excessive dependence on foreign finance, have been severely hit as foreign investors deleveraged and capital flows dried up. Thus, recent experience suggests a cautious approach to the pace and scope of capital account liberalisation as there is a strong linkage among capital account liberalisation, domestic financial sector reform, and the design of monetary and exchange rate policy.

Funding of Banking Sector in Emerging Market Economies: It is evident from the crisis that banks–whether foreign or local–played a major role in the origination or in the transmission of the crisis. According to BIS (2009b), "weakness in major foreign banks, and their need to retrench, was certainly a factor. The presence of local banks funded by domestic deposits, by contrast, generally seems to have helped the diversification of risk and made banking systems more resilient to a foreign shock". It has been found that banks that rely heavily on wholesale funding are naturally more vulnerable to any shock of market liquidity. Excessive dependence of entities on wholesale funding markets is an issue of systemic concern and needs a cautious approach. When loans are larger than deposits, banks resort to funding from foreign parents or domestic and international wholesale markets to finance the gap.

Thus, it is not a surprise that in the eastern European EMEs, viz., Hungary, Romania and the Ukraine, where the stress has been more acute, the loan-to-deposit ratios were all greater than one.

Likewise, it was observed that foreign banks presence was associated with currency mismatches. For instance, in central and Eastern Europe, foreign banks extended Euro and Swiss franc-denominated corporate, home, and car loans to firms and households with incomes in local currency, which eventually aggravated the corporate and household financial distress when local currencies depreciated. This indicates that emerging markets, while encouraging foreign bank entry, simultaneously strictly regulate their local lending practices.

Future Challenges for EMEs Including India
Need for Development of Local Bond Market in EMEs: The issues with regard to banking-sector intermediation during recent crisis highlight the need for further development of local bond markets in EMEs. As the financial crisis curtailed the ability of borrowers in emerging markets to find funds

abroad, they had to turn to domestic markets in order to raise funds. Local-currency bond markets had already grown tremendously since the crisis of the 1990s. It is emphasized that deepening local currency bond markets should now be a top priority for emerging economies. Bond markets provide an alternative to bank intermediation. According to Eichengreen (2009c), there is evidence that countries with better-developed bond markets experienced less negative fallout from the crisis as large firms, in particular, retained access to non-bank sources of finance.

These firms were able to finance their operations at longer-term tenors, thus obviating the need to go back to the markets once conditions deteriorated. It is evident that local currency bond markets are becoming an alternative funding source in several emerging economies. These markets have grown rapidly, doubling in size from US$ 2.2 trillion in 2003 to US$ 5.5 trillion at the end of 2008. In fact, learning from the previous crises of the 1990s, emerging markets' governments have sought to develop local-currency bond markets to help prevent a re-run of the string of financial crises, particularly like the 1997 Asian financial crisis. East Asian countries have been at the forefront of bond market development (Dalla and Hesse, 2009). These markets are playing an important role in the provision of finance to emerging-market governments and corporations, which are largely shut out of international financial markets during the global financial crisis, and in reducing their dependence on the banking sector.

With reduced currency mismatches, most Latin American and Asian economies did indeed prove to be resilient during the crisis. According to Braasch (2009), local-currency bond markets served as a "spare tyre" in some EMEs and developing countries. In many emerging markets, by helping to correct currency and maturity mismatches, local currency bond markets contributed to financial stability. Even though some progress has been made in EMEs in terms of developing corporate bond markets, there are still issues with regard to size, lack of market-based yield curve, difficulties with proper disclosure of accounting information and weakness in corporate governance. Thus, countries, which are still at an early stage of domestic bond market development, should focus on building the market infrastructure of the primary market while those at an advanced stage of corporate bond market development need to undertake efficiency based reforms. With deeper local markets, more borrowing and lending can take place within a country's borders, perhaps reducing the incentive to go abroad. It is, argued that further deepening of local-currency bond markets would help reduce the probability that currency depreciation can transform into a full-blown financial crisis.

Need for a Counter-cyclical Fiscal Policy Framework: One of the consequences of the financial crisis has been the transfer of financial risks to fiscal authorities, combined with the financing burden of fiscal stimulus. However, it remains to be seen as to what extent the fiscal stimulus packages undertaken by various advanced and emerging economies, produce an impact beyond the short-term support to demand and generate a positive impact on long-term potential growth. In addition, expansionary fiscal policies have raised concerns over the crowding out of investment in the private sector and the sustainability of public sector finances in a number of countries. This, in turn, may have implications for the nascent recovery that seems to be taking place. Furthermore, the possibility cannot be ruled out that a vicious circle, with rising debt levels holding back growth and pushing interest rates up, will develop over the medium-term. Thus, many countries could face the challenge of mitigating this risk by designing and articulating medium-term fiscal consolidation plans that take into account their financial sector stabilization policies.

It observed that fiscal deficits have surged in most of the economies as policymakers have sought to counteract weakness in aggregate demand and revive their financial systems. For instance, in case of advanced economies, fiscal authorities have responded to the crisis by offering capital to support central bank programmes, purchasing illiquid assets (for instance, in the US) and providing guarantees to encourage securities origination (as in the UK). Such measures, along with aggressive monetary policy easing during the crisis, helped contain the rise in the cost of borrowing for the private and public sectors. In fact, most mature market economies running significant fiscal deficits have been able to limit the increase in domestic interest rates by tapping foreign savings from emerging market central banks, oil exporters, and sovereign wealth funds.

As a result, it is widely expected that the major advanced as well as emerging economies will emerge from the crisis with heavy public deficits and rapidly mounting debt. According to an estimate by the IMF (2009e), the average fiscal deficit of the advanced G-20 countries is projected to be around 10 and 8.5 percent of GDP in 2009 and 2010, respectively. If foreign investors become concerned about long-term fiscal sustainability in these countries, interest rates on government securities would need to adjust higher and the exchange rate would depreciate. More recently, the belief that a country can borrow without any limits is questioned after the episode of Greece. This is a reminder that fiscal space cannot be overextended.

In order to attenuate the impact of the financial crisis, emerging economies should be supported by large fiscal stimulus measures. EMEs that entered the crisis with more policy space and less binding financing constraints were able to react more aggressively with fiscal and monetary policy. Even the recovery process was faster in EMEs that gave a bigger fiscal stimulus, had stronger pre-crisis fundamentals, and had faster growing trading partners (IMF, 2010b). In fact, Asia's fiscal response (in terms of GDP) has been larger than in an average G-20 country (Kato, 2009). One of the major findings from the research on the crisis is that countries, which were able to conduct counter-cyclical policies, were also able to withstand the crisis better.

However, many emerging and developing countries lacked the 'policy' and 'fiscal' space to deal with the global economic crisis. As a result, there are large asymmetries in global economic policies. According to Cavallo (2009), "the lucky ones that earned the chance of conducting counter-cyclical policies were those that had previously resisted the temptation of taking comfort in favourable tailwinds and had prepared for the rainy day." It observed that countries, which could not create fiscal space for counter-cyclical policies during the upturn, had little room for independent policy actions during the crisis. Thus, the crisis presents a case for further strengthening of their fiscal correction and consolidation process during the boom period to create fiscal space for undertaking effective counter-cyclical fiscal measures during a downturn or recessionary phase. The recreation of fiscal and policy space for emerging and developing countries on a sustainable basis need to be a central feature of the reform agenda. This is now clearer after the recent events in some parts of Europe.

Need for Social Security System in EMEs : Although the major emerging market economies like China and India were moderately affected by the recent crisis, it is perceived that the pace of reduction in poverty alleviation programmes suffer in many other developing countries. Undoubtedly, these countries were affected first by rising food and oil prices and then by recent crisis, which could have played a key role in boosting global demand and supporting global recovery, but they need access to finance for years to come. Taking cognizance of the potential demand that these countries have, policymakers in these countries need to initiate measures towards setting up and strengthening the social safety nets.

It is noted that some of the best social protection programmes in the world have emerged during times of macroeconomic stress. EMEs like China and India not been affected much during the recent crisis due to a number of reasons, but in the period ahead their trade and financial integration with advanced markets is expected to grow further. Thus, such resilience to external shocks is unlikely to guarantee. In such a scenario, it becomes important, albeit challenging, for emerging and developing countries to gradually put in place an effective social security system. Not only will it help the automatic stabilizers to work better but it will also attenuate the need for undertaking sudden large-scale discretionary fiscal policy measures. Besides these, pursuing such structural policies in countries that have excessive current account surpluses can help to hold global imbalances at a sustainable level. An improvement in the social security system and financial markets may decrease private savings in such countries.

Self-insurance against Future Crisis: The recent crisis and its impact on EMEs has led to a debate on whether countries should seek to self-insure against future crises by building up their foreign exchange reserves in order to better prepare for future crises. According to IMF (2010b), higher international reserves holdings, by reducing external vulnerability, help buffer the impact of the crisis. However, reserves had diminishing returns: at very high levels of reserves, there is little discernable evidence of their moderating impact on output collapse. In this context, there are two contrasting arguments. Blanchard et al. (2009) are of the view that it is difficult to conclude whether this self-insurance was indeed successful. Although most emerging markets survived the recent crisis better than in the past, it could be attributed to the fact that, first, the crisis originated in advanced economies, and second, to much better macroeconomic policies and frameworks in emerging economies than in the past. Highlighting this, they argue that even though Brazil has much higher reserves than Mexico, even in terms of GDP, there has been very little difference in the performance of credit default swap spreads. In short, markets did not see Mexico as more vulnerable than Brazil despite its huge reserves.

Truman (2009) is of the opinion that seeking self-insurance through reserve accumulation could be a wrong lesson to learn from the global crisis. In his view, countries should self-insure against future crises by putting in place, as best as they can, robust economic and financial policy frameworks. One element of that type of self-insurance should be adequate holdings of foreign exchange reserves, but that alone is insufficient. Large holdings of foreign exchange reserves provide an expensive buffer against a global financial crisis. Citing the case of South Korea, which had foreign exchange reserves of US$ 264 billion in February 2008, he concluded that building up foreign exchange reserves does not guarantee self-insurance.

During the crisis, it was the gross inflows together with gross outflows that mattered rather than the net surplus on the current account or the net accumulation of international reserves. Further, the sources of foreign exchange reserves are an important factor in determining their durability as an instrument of self-insurance. However, Truman agrees that Korea would have suffered more if it had large current account deficits in the period before the crisis, or if it had held negligible foreign exchange reserves when the crisis hit, but its huge reserve holdings alone were inadequate to self-insure Korea from the crisis. In short, building up of foreign exchange may not be the sole factor for self-insurance. It should be accompanied by putting in place a sound economic and financial policy framework. The Global Financial Safety Net (GFSN) Expert Group has deliberated on these issues under the G-20 forum.

India's comfortable foreign exchange reserves provided confidence in its ability to manage balance of payments notwithstanding lower export demand and dampened capital flows (Subbarao, 2009a). In the absence of a sufficient cushion of foreign exchange reserves, perhaps arresting the pressure on the exchange rate would have been very challenging. In this context, it noted that the tendency towards self-insurance by accumulating foreign currency reserves in EMEs has its roots in a less-than-adequate response from multilateral financial institutions like the IMF. Experiencing a lack of financial support during the East Asian crisis, EMEs tended to accumulate foreign exchange reserves in order to gain some insulation from future crises.

During the recent crisis, the willingness of the Federal Reserve to extend swaps to central banks around the world, ensuring provision of liquidity directly to other central banks, perhaps indirectly, implies the need for large foreign exchange reserves built up by individual central banks as a buffer in times of crisis. The need for self-insurance can, however, be reduced with effective mechanisms for liquidity provisioning and reserve management at the international level, both regionally and multilaterally. Another important lesson for EMEs from the crisis is that the corner hypothesis postulating that countries should be moving to one or another corner in the choice of exchange rate regimes, viz., fully flexible or fixed exchange rates, is out and intermediate regimes are the order of the day.

Concluding Observations

To conclude, recent developments clearly raise an issue whether EMEs can protect themselves against the transmission of a large financial shock in advanced economies. It appears that reducing individual country vulnerabilities by improving current account and fiscal balances may not have fully insulated them from the transmission of financial stress but improvement on these parameters along with strong policy frameworks definitely provides greater headroom for implementation of an appropriate domestic policy response in such situations and facilitates faster recovery. Similarly, the crisis has taught an important lesson that forex market intervention to contain sharp, disruptive depreciation is no longer a sin, and reserves are a new virtue. Thus, it is felt that any framework of global financial safety net should have three principal pillars: one, a domestic financial safety net comprising a robust international reserve position and prudential framework; two, regional financial safety nets consisting of regional swap pools and bilateral swap pools; and three, global safety net encompassing a wider role for multilateral institutions.

It can be concluded that the causes of the crisis have helped us draw lessons, the implementation of which, however, could be a challenging task for policymaking bodies at the national and international levels. It seems that the lessons of earlier crises motivated some emerging economies to strengthen budgets, reduce public debts, limit current account deficits, and more carefully manage foreign currency exposures, resulting in reduced vulnerabilities and increased policy space. This proved to be profoundly advantageous during the recent crisis, Nonetheless, for the EMEs, the key message from the recent crisis is with regard to continuation of sound policy frameworks in the financial sector, generating adequate investment capacities to balance global demand, continued efforts towards fiscal consolidation to have better room for discretionary policy in future and reviewing their approach towards capital account liberalisation.

Global developments in the recent period have strengthened the argument that EMEs cannot immunize themselves from the repercussions of a crisis originating in advanced economies. However, the impact could be moderated by undertaking sound policy measures in the financial and fiscal sectors. In order to achieve better sustainability of their growth momentum, EMEs, inter alia, need to enhance the absorptive capacities of their economies. This is required not only for raising their growth potential but also for balancing global demand and better absorption of capital inflows. Furthermore, the crisis has drawn attention to the issue of capital account management by the EMEs. The list of lessons from the crisis may not be exhaustive or fully conclusive.

Nonetheless, they unravel a number of issues that need to be debated by policymakers at the national and global level. Whilst the recent crisis may prompt fundamental changes to economic regulations given the interconnection between markets beyond national boundaries, national solutions may no longer suffice. By requiring international co-operation on macroeconomic policies, trade and financial regulations, the recent financial crisis may more importantly provide an opportunity for countries to take the first step towards the consensus required to address far deeper global problems. Recent crisis also provides an opportune time to gather the political will to put in place long-needed structural reforms, nationally as well globally. Lessons drawn from the crisis need to be prioritized and translated into action by policymakers in a harmonized manner so as to minimise the possibility of such crisis in future.

References
Andritzky et al. 2009, "Policies to Mitigate Procyclicality", IMF Staff Position Note No. SPN/09/09, International Monetary Fund, May.

Bank for International Settlement, 2009, "Capital flows and EMEs", CGFS Papers No. 33, Report submitted by a Working Group established by the Committee on the Global Financial System. January 2009, 79th Annual Report, 1 April 2008-31 March 2009.

Bernanke, Ben S. 2009b, "Financial Reform to Address Systemic Risk", Remarks at the Council on Foreign Relations, Washington, D.C., March 10, 2009.

Bernanke, Ben S., 2010, "Monetary Policy and the Housing Bubble", Speech at the Annual Meeting of the American Economic Association, Atlanta, Georgia on January 3, 2010.

Blanchard, Olivier, Hamid Faruqee and Vladimir Klyuev, 2009, "Did Foreign Reserves Help Weather the Crisis?" IMF Survey Magazine, October 8, 2009.

Bordo, Michael D. and Olivier Jeanne, 2002, "Boom-Busts in Asset Prices, Economic Instability, and Monetary Policy", NBER Working Paper No. 8966.

Braasch, Bernd, 2009, "How have local currency bond markets weathered the financial crisis?" Paper presented at 4th OECD Forum on African Global Debt Management, November 12-13, 2009.

Cavallo, Eduardo and Alejandro Izquierdo, 2009, "Dealing with the Crisis: Lessons for Latin America", http://www.iadb.org/res/publications/pubfiles/pubRIT-164.pdf.

Dalla, Ismail and Hesse, Heiko, 2009, "Rapidly growing local-currency bond markets offer a viable alternative funding source for emerging-market issuers" available at http://www.voxeu.org/ index.php? q=node/4081.

Eichengreen, Barry, 2009c, "Lessons of the Crisis for Emerging Markets", ADBI Working Paper Series, No. 179, December 2009.

G-30 Report on Financial Reform: A Framework for Financial Stability.

Gerdesmeier, Dieter; Hans-Eggert Reimers and Barbara Roffia, 2009, "Asset Price Misalignments and the Role of Money and Credit", ECB Working Paper Series No. 1068, July.

International Monetary Fund, 2009a, "Lessons of the Financial Crisis for Future Regulation of Financial Institutions and Markets and for Liquidity Management." Paper prepared by Monetary and Capital Markets Department of IMF, February 4, 2009.

——2009b, "Initial Lessons of Crisis", Paper prepared by Monetary and Capital Markets Department of IMF, February 6, 2009.

——2009d, World Economic Outlook, April 2009.

——2009e, Global Financial Stability Report, October 2009.

——2010b, How Did Emerging Markets Cope in the Crisis?, Prepared by the Strategy, Policy, and Review Department, IMF, Washington, D.C., June 2010.

Issing, O., 2002, "Monetary Policy in a Changing Environment", contribution to the Symposium on "Rethinking Stabilization Policy", hosted by the Federal Reserve Bank of Kansas City (Jackson Hole, 30 August 2002).

Kato, Takatoshi, 2009, "Impact of the Global Financial Crisis and Its Implications for the East Asian Economy." Keynote Speech by Deputy Managing Director, International Monetary Fund at the First International Conference of Korea International Financial Association, Seoul, Korea, October 16, 2009.

Mishkin, Frederic S., 2008, "How Should We Respond to Asset

Price Bubbles?" Remarks at the Wharton Financial Institutions Centre and Oliver Wyman Institute's Annual Financial Risk Roundtable, Philadelphia, Pennsylvania, May 15, 2008.

Mohan, Rakesh and Muneesh Kapur, 2010, "Liberalization and Regulation of Capital Flows: Lessons for Emerging Market Economies", ADBI Working Paper Series, No. 186.

Nijathaworn, Bandid, 2009, "The Recent Global Crisis, Lessons Learned, and Future Implications." Keynote address at the 11th SEACEN Conference of Directors of Supervision of Asia-Pacific Economies, Bangkok of the Bank of Thailand, July 29, 2009.

Orphanides, Athanasios, 2010, "Monetary Policy Lessons from the Crisis", CEPR Discussion Paper No. 7891, June.

Ostry, Jonathan D.; Atish R. Ghosh; Karl Habermeier; Marcos Chamon; Mahvash S. Qureshi; and Dennis B.S. Reinhardt, (2010), "Capital Inflows: The Role of Controls", IMF Staff Position Note SPN/10/04, February 19.

Papademos, Lucas, 2009, "Monetary Policy and the 'Great Crisis': Lessons and Challenges." Speech by Vice President of the ECB at the 37th Economics Conference "Beyond the Crisis: Economic Policy in a New Macroeconomic Environment" organised by the Österreichische National bank, Vienna, May 14, 2009.

Reddy, Y.V., 2009, "India's Financial Sector in Current Times", S. Guhan Memorial Lecture, October 22, 2009.

Report of G-20 Working Group on Reforming the IMF, March 2009.

Report of G-20 Working Group on Enhancing Sound Regulation and Strengthening Transparency, March 2009.

Report of the High-level Group on Financial Supervision in the EU, (Chairman: Jacques de Larosière), February 2009.

Strauss-Kahn, Dominique, 2009b, "Take-Off or Holding Pattern? Prospects for the Global Economy", An Address to the Confederation of British Industry Annual Conference by Dominique Strauss-Kahn, Managing Director, International Monetary Fund, London, November 23, 2009.

Subbarao, D., 2009a, "Risk Management in the Midst of the Global Financial Crisis", RBI Bulletin, June.

Subbarao, D., 2009c, "Challenges for the Central Banks" Remarks at the Panel Discussion organised at Hyderabad as part of RBI's Platinum Jubilee Celebration, August 14, 2009.

Subbarao, D., 2009d, "Financial Stability: Issues and Challenges", RBI Bulletin, October.

Subramanian, Arvind and John Willamson, 2009b, "Brazil Warns Against Foreign Finance Fetish." Business Standard, October 30, 2009.

Tarullo, Daniel K., 2009, "Regulatory Reform", Testimony before the Committee on Financial Services, U.S. House of Representatives, Washington, D.C., October 29, 2009.

Taylor, John B., 2010, "Lessons from the Financial Crisis for Monetary Policy in Emerging Markets", L. K. Jha Memorial Lecture given at the Platinum Jubilee Celebration of the Reserve Bank of India in Mumbai on February 24, 2010.

Truman, Edwin M., 2009, "The Global Financial Crisis: Lessons Learned and Challenges for Developing Countries", Remarks at the Eighteenth Cycle of Economics Lectures, Banco de Guatemala, June 16, 2009.

Turner, Adair, 2010, "After the Crises: Assessing the Costs and Benefits of Financial Liberalisation", Speech at 14th Chintaman Deshmukh Memorial Lecture, Reserve Bank of India, Mumbai on February 24, 2010.

World Bank, 2009, Global Monitoring Report 2009: A Development Emergency. Washington D.C: World Bank.

8

Global Financial Crisis and the Developing Countries

R. Narayanan

Introduction

The current financial crisis has evolved differently from other major crises that have hit the developing world in recent decades. Not only is it occurring in a world of unprecedented financial globalization, where the financial sector plays a historically large role in economic activity, but it is also an "imported" crisis, with origins outside the developing world. The crisis also comes on the heels of a major global shock from high food and fuel prices that has imposed a heavy economic burden on many countries and significantly increased the incidence of poverty and vulnerability.

The uniqueness of the current configuration of economic challenges has important implications for the nature and effectiveness of the policy options available to developing country governments. It implies that the policy responses of individual developing countries are unlikely to measurably affect the depth and length of the global crisis. However, their actions can affect the impact of the crisis on their own economies. Policymakers need to be ready to react forcibly and quickly at the first signs of domestic weakness, including the rapid involvement of external assistances necessary. More generally, countries need to maintain sound macroeconomic and financial-sector policies, while focusing on mitigating the potential negative impacts of the crisis on those living at the margin. The unprecedented scope of the crisis calls for innovative solutions to complement those more traditional policies that have a sound record of success under similar circumstances.

Many developing countries are moving into a new danger zone, with heightened risk to exports, investment, credit, banking systems, budgets, the balance of payments, and the most vulnerable. With this latest financial crisis, growth is likely to weaken even more sharply. Developing country exports to developed countries are falling, capital is being withdrawn from emerging markets and short-term credit is drying up. This could trigger a fall in production and investment by the productive sector. Sharp and tighter credit conditions and weak growth is likely to cut into government revenues and government's ability to spend, to meet education, health and gender goals.

Countries dependent on exports, remittances or foreign investment, exhibiting high current account deficits or rising inflation, and those with extensive fuel/food subsidies are most vulnerable to a sharp slowdown—especially if accompanied by significant tightening of financial market conditions. Coming on the heels of the food and fuel price shock, the global financial crisis could significantly set back the fight against poverty.

Rejection of De-coupling Hypothesis

The decoupling hypothesis—which was intellectually fashionable prior to the start of the crisis—held that even if advanced economies went into a downturn, emerging economies will remain unscathed because of their substantial foreign exchange reserves, improved policy framework, robust corporate balance sheets and relatively healthy banking sector. In a rapidly globalizing world, the decoupling hypothesis was never totally persuasive. Given the experience of the post-Crisis period, the decoupling hypothesis stands invalidated. Reinforcing the notion that in a globalised world no country can be an island, growth prospects of emerging economies have been undermined by the cascading financial crisis with, of course, considerable variation across countries.

Inter-sectoral Contagion: Till recently, there was a view that the fallout of the crisis will remain confined to the financial sector and that, at the most, there would only be a shallow recession in the advanced economies. These expectations, as it now turns out, have been belied. The contagion has traversed from the financial to the real sector and it now looks like the recession will be deeper and the recovery longer than earlier anticipated.

Inter-country Contagion: Economic malaises are contagious. A crisis of such magnitude in developed countries is bound to have an impact around the world. Most emerging market economies have slowed down significantly. India too has been affected. In these difficult times, when most economies are struggling to stay afloat, a healthy 6 to 7 percent rate of GDP growth still makes India (after China) the second fastest growing economy in the world.

Contagion and Developing Countries: Monetary policy developments in the leading economies not only affect developing countries domestically, but also have a profound impact on the rest of the world through changes in risk premia and search for yield, leading to significant switches in capital flows. While the large volatility in the monetary policy in the US could have been dictated by internal compulsions to maintain employment and price stability, the consequent volatility in capital flows impinges on exchange rate movements and more generally on asset and commodity prices. The monetary policy dynamics of the advanced economies thus involve sharp adjustments for the developing countries.

Private capital flows to developing countries including India have grown rapidly since the 1980s, but with increased volatility over time. Large capital flows to the developing countries can be attributed to a variety of push and pull factors. The pull factors that have led to higher capital flows in these countries have included the following: (a) strong growth over the past decade, (b) reduction in inflation, (c) macroeconomic stability, (d) opening up of capital accounts, and (e) buoyant growth prospects.

The major push factor is the stance of monetary policy in the advanced economies. Periods of loose monetary policy coupled with search for yield in the advanced economies encourages large capital inflows to developing countries and vice versa in periods of tighter monetary policy. Thus, swings in monetary policy in the advanced economies lead to cycles and volatility in capital flows to developing countries. Innovations in information technology have also contributed to the two-way movement in capital flows. In response to these factors, capital flows to developing countries since the early 1980s have grown over time, but with large volatility.

As regards the nature of foreign investment, while direct investment flows have generally seen a steady increase over the period, portfolio flows as well as other private flows have exhibited substantial volatility. While direct investment flows largely reflect the pull factors, portfolio and bank flows reflect both the push and the pull factors. It is also evident that capital account transactions have grown much faster relative to current account transactions, and gross capital flows are a multiple of both net capital flows and current account transactions. Also, large private capital flows have taken place in an environment when developing countries have been witnessing current account surpluses leading to substantial accumulation of foreign exchange reserves in many of these economies.

Relative Resilience Exhibited by Developing Countries

In contrast to the previous episodes of global turmoil, developing countries, especially India, have exhibited relative resilience, though equity market and exchange rate pressures have intensified in recent times. So far, the investment sentiment is positive for most Asian developing countries, reflecting their strong economic performance and, for some countries, favourable investment opportunities. Credit policy reforms, better structuring of banking sector debt and improved fiscal positions have also played their role making these economies resilient from the crisis. In addition, large foreign exchange reserves, particularly in Asia, also provide a degree of protection against possible sudden stops. Another factor that could be of relevance for this favourable situation is the relatively smaller presence of foreign banks in the Asian banking sector. This is evident from the fact that the share of banking assets held by foreign banks in these economies generally lies between 0 and 10 percent.

In spite of the fact that no significant macroeconomic disruption has taken place in developing countries, some vulnerabilities do exist. There are indications that the current crisis will have some implications in terms of higher funding costs and raising external finance, particularly for lower-rated firms. Further, countries with significant foreign bank presence might be vulnerable to financial stress faced by a parent bank. Similarly, slowdown in advanced countries might impact the remittances to developing countries.

The Central and East European economies seem to have suffered the brunt of the global financial markets upheaval, given their large current account deficits. Banks in most of these countries are in need of government support in the form of recapitalisation.

Several emerging Eastern European countries, including Hungary, Romania and Ukraine, have sought IMF support to stabilise their financial markets. The emerging economies of Europe which saw plummeting valuations in equity markets include the Czech Republic, Hungary, Poland and Russia. During 2008-09, the foreign exchange markets of most emerging market economies continued to be under pressure. The Russian rouble continued the downward spiral against both the US dollar and the Euro.

Some other currencies that suffered sharp losses during the period include the Czech koruna, the Hungarian forint, the Polish zloty, the Brazilian real, the Korean won, the Mexican peso and the Indonesian rupiah

Though emerging market economies, including India, do not have direct or significant exposure to stressed financial instruments or troubled financial institutions, they are not immune to the adverse effects of the financial crisis.

Economic Context

The global financial crisis that emerged in September 2008, following more than a year of financial turmoil, will have serious implications around the globe. Developing countries were at first sheltered from the worst elements of the turmoil, but this is no longer the case, as the cyclical downturn that was already under way has intensified. Financial conditions have become much tighter, capital flows to developing countries have dried up, and huge amounts of capital have been withdrawn, leading to sharp falls in equity valuations and increases in bond spreads. As of mid-October, developing country enquiry markets had given up almost all of their gains since the beginning of 2008 and initial public offerings had disappeared. Spreads on sovereign bonds and commercial debt (which until recently had been the most important source of developing country finance) have risen sharply. Bank lending is also down and foreign direct investment inflows are expected to decline in the final quarter of the year.

Virtually no country, developing or industrial, has escaped the impact of the widening crisis, although those countries with stronger fundamentals and less integration into the global economy going into the crisis have generally been less affected. The deterioration in financing conditions has been most severe for countries with large current accounts deficits, and for those that showed signs of overheating and unsustainably rapid credit growth prior to the intensification of the financial crisis. Of the 20 developing countries whose economies have reacted most sharply to the deterioration in conditions (as measured by exchange rate depreciation, increase in spreads, equity market declines and large current account deficits), seven come from Europe and Central Asia, and eight from Latin America. And as a knock-on effect, with the crisis taking its toll on even the most well off countries, there is a serious risk that some donors might consider stepping back from aid commitments when they are most needed.

Consensus growth projections for developed countries in 2009 are being slashed and world trade volumes may fall for the first time since the 1982 recession. The consequent downturn in developing country exports will be the widespread shock generated by the crisis and private capital flows to developing countries are likely to fall significantly in 2009, led by pull-backs in portfolio flows and international bank lending. On the positive side, improvements in macro economic policies in developing countries over the past decade (e.g., more sustainable fiscal policies, build-up of large foreign exchange reserves) especially in large countries, suggest that unsustainable levels of sovereign debt are likely to be less of an issue in the initial stages than in previous crisis. But, if fiscal positions deteriorate under the impact of the crisis, sovereign debt burdens may increase rapidly, and access to international capital markets may become more of a constraint.

Earlier concerns about rapid credit growth in some developing countries have been proven valid. Large portfolio and foreign bank lending flows have contributed to rapid growth in credit to the private sector and large private sector driven current account deficits in a number of countries. The sudden deceleration of inflows will force a sharp adjustment in private sector activity. There is a high probability of balance sheet deterioration and possible banking crisis where banks and non-bank financial institutions have expended credit to the private sector most rapidly. There may be an especially direct channel in economies where there has been substantial borrowing from foreign banks, either through branches in the domestic market or through borrowing by local banks. Central and Eastern European economies, which have experienced especially rapid credit increases, with foreign banks playing a dominant role in the domestic market, could be most at risk.

Investment is expected to suffer as it bears much of the direct impact of the financial crisis. Investment was the main driving force for developing country growth over the past 5 years, contributing almost half of the increase in domestic demand. For 2008, investment is expected to increase only moderately in middle-income countries, compared with 13 percent growth in 2007. There is a risk that investment in developing countries may be headed for a "perfect storm" with a convergence of slowing world growth, withdrawal of equity and term lending from the private sector, and higher interest rates, with a further risk that lower commodity prices in the medium term will deter new investment in natural resource sectors.

Should the freeze in credit markets not thaw quickly enough, then the consequences for developing countries could be severe. Financing conditions would deteriorate rapidly, and otherwise sound domestic financial sectors could find themselves unable to borrow or unwilling to lend both internationally and domestically, and domestic productive sectors would be deprived of working and long-term capital. Such a scenario would be characterized by a long and profound recession in high-income countries and substantial disruption and turmoil, including bank failures and currency crises in a wide range of developing countries.

Corporate with high leverage or reliance on trade finance, swaps and other financial instruments are particularly vulnerable. Sharply negative growth in a number of developing countries and all of the attendant repercussions, including increased poverty and unemployment, would be inevitable. If steps that are being taken to restore the functioning of capital markets and maintain the flow of credit to the productive sector succeed, a milder downturn is possible, with the economic dislocation contained mainly within the financial sector.

Remittances from host countries are expected to be decline in response to the global slowdown but the impact on flows to recipient countries will depend significantly on exchange rates. In 28 countries, remittance to developing countries was larger than revenue from the most important commodity export, and in 36 countries they were larger than private and public capital inflows. They are also a powerful poverty reduction mechanism. For example, in Nicaragua, remittances reduce poverty incidence by four percentage points on average, and five percentage points in urban areas. In Albania, households with migrants to Italy and Greece have an incidence of poverty that is half the national rate (i.e., 15 and 19 percent compared to an average of 32 percent).

Remittance flows from host to developing countries, which reached an estimated US$ 295 billion in 2008, began slowing down in the second half of 2008 and in 2009. The global slowdown is also expected to lead to a sharp reduction in employment opportunities in the developed world, especially in sectors with a high concentration of migrants (e.g., construction, retail, catering). This plus lower oil revenues in Gulf countries, will lead to a decline in migrant earnings. However, the large exchange rate fluctuations of recent months have dwarfed the expected changes in remittances denominated in host-country currencies. As a result, changes in the local currency value of remittances would vary widely by country. Overall, remittance flows into developing countries are expected to decline from 2.0 to 1.7 percent of recipient country GDP.

Low-income countries (LIC's) will be significantly affected by the crisis even though the channels of transactions are likely quite different from those operating in emerging markets. Financial sectors in LIC's are less integrated into global financial markets. As a result, the direct impact of the crisis is likely to be more limited. Nevertheless, LIC's will be impacted through slower export growth (global trade is projected to decline in 2009), reduced remittances, lower commodity prices (which will reduce incomes in commodity exporters) and the potential for reduced aid from donors. The crisis may also lead to a reduction in private investment flows, making weak economies even less able to cope with internal vulnerabilities and development needs.

Impact of the Food and Fuel Price Shocks

Recently, amidst historically high food and fuel prices, the global community's attention was focused on the impact of these shocks on poor countries and populations. The rise in food prices between 2005 and early 2007 was estimated to have increased the share of the population of East Asia, the Middle East, and South Asia living in extreme poverty by at least 1 percentage point, a setback equivalent to seven years of progress towards meeting the poverty MDG. The impact on the urban poor was particularly acute, increasing the incidence of poverty by more than 1.5 percentage points in East Asia, the Middle Asia, and Sub-Saharan Africa.

As a result of the food and fuel crisis, the number of extremely poor was estimated to have increased by at least 100 million. The poverty deficit (the annual cost of lifting the incomes of all the poor to the poverty line) rose by US$ 38 billion or 0.5 percent of developing country GDP. The increase in the number of poor due to the food crisis was only part of the story. Equally worrisome was that many of those already poor are slipping even more deeply into poverty. Recent estimates of poverty depth (i.e., the gap in consumption between the average poor household and the poverty line) show that the poverty is deepening, with the extreme poor being hit hardest. Eighty-eight percent of the increase in urban poverty depth from rising food prices is from households becoming poorer and only 12 percent from households falling into poverty.

Recent decline in food and fuel prices do not imply that pressures and problems have disappeared. For the very poor, reducing consumption from already very low levels, even for a short period, can have important long-term consequences. The poorest households may have had to reduce the quantity and/or quality of the food, schooling, and basic services they consumed, leading to irreparable damage to the health and education of millions of children. Poor households forced to switch from more expensive to cheaper and less nutritional foodstuffs, or cut back on total calorie intake altogether, face weight loss and severe malnutrition. Already during 2008, higher food prices have increased the number of children suffering permanent cognitive and physical injury due to malnutrition by 44 million. Regardless of recent decline in global food and fuel prices, this represents a tragic loss of human and economic potential. Many of the countries most exposed to rising global food and fuel prices are those with high pre-existing levels of malnutrition. Burundi, Madagascar, Niger, Timor Leste and Yemen are among the ten most affected for both stunting and wasting indicators. All of these countries experienced double-digit food inflation in 2007-08.

Second round impacts on inflation remain a concern. Until recently, rising commodity prices and tight capacity in many countries were causing both headline and core inflation to pick up throughout the world, with headline inflation rising by some five percentage points among developing countries. However, even with world commodity prices falling back considerably and capacity pressures easing, inflation risks remain. In many countries, consumer prices may prove to be less flexible downwards and upward pressure on prices remain as households seek to recoup the significant real-income losses endured since January 2007 and firms strive to restore profitability. The combination of these price pressures with slowing growth and rising unemployment raises the spectre of stagflation.

The food and fuel price shocks have already imposed large fiscal costs on developing countries, undermining their ability to respond to fall-out from the financial crisis. Policymakers responding to high food and fuel prices have made extensive use of tax reductions to offset higher prices and increased spending on subsidies and income support. Data from a recent IMF survey covering 161 countries shows that nearly 57 percent of countries reduced taxes on food while 27 percent increased fuel subsidies. The reliance on "across the board" tax reductions and subsidies is unfortunate because these measures are often more regressive, more costly and more difficult to reform once in place. Fuel subsidies are usually much more regressive than food subsidies and often have further adverse environment consequence. Reliance on inefficient fiscal measures such as untargeted subsides is also regrettable given the need to create the fiscal space to accommodate a permanent increase in the size of targeted safety nets. Careful fiscal planning is needed to protect critical growth enhancing spending, prune low-priority expenditures and ensure fiscal sustainability in the medium term. These pressures will only increase as the global financial crisis takes it toll.

The sharp turn around in commodity prices may require equally dramatic adjustment among commodity exporters. While the terms of trade deterioration faced by food and fuel importers has begun to reverse, exporters of these commodities are facing sharp declines in prices with potentially large implications for their current accounts. At the same time, a large group of developing countries have become heavily reliant on foreign financing in recent years, whether in the form of aid or private capital flows. Around half of all developing countries have current account deficits in excess of 5 percent of GDP and about one third have current account deficits of over 10 percents of GDP. Should the current extreme liquidity squeeze persist, it is bound to have repercussions for global growth and the capacity of countries to obtain external finance. There is evidence of this already.

World Response to the Crisis

The sub-prime crisis that emerged in the US housing

mortgage market in the second half of 2007 snowballed into a global financial and economic crisis. The global financial landscape changed significantly during the course of 2008-09 wherein several large international financial institutions either failed or were restructured, with the support of very large government interventions in many countries, to prevent imminent collapse. The significant deterioration in global financial conditions since mid-September 2008, led to severe disruptions in the short-term funding markets, widening of risk spreads, sharp fall in equity prices and inactivity in the markets for asset-backed securities.

Resultantly, the strain on the balance sheets of financial institutions increased, threatening the viability of some of the most well-known financial entities in the world. The freezing up of credit markets necessitated extraordinary actions on the part of central banks and governments in countries across the world to mitigate the risks posed by the financial crisis.

Bailout Packages: As the market mayhem manifested in terms of crisis of confidence, resulting in drying up of liquidity, governments and central banks stepped in to restore confidence and assure relief to the beleaguered institutions. Alarmed by the financial catastrophe, governments worldwide led by US, announced bailout packages to control the landslide.

To stabilize financial markets and revive credit and capital flows, a number of measures were undertaken by countries across the world. For example, the US Government sanctioned US$ 700 billion under the Troubled Assets Relief Programme to strengthen the US financial market. Besides injecting a substantial amount of liquidity into the system, policy interest rates were cut by almost all countries. Major central banks decided to ease monetary conditions as inflationary pressures appeared to have receded consequent on decline in international energy and commodity prices.

As the epicentre of the global financial crisis was the US, Fed rate was reduced in stages to 1 percent while European

Central Bank cut the short-term rate twice to reach the rate of 3 percent. The Reserve Bank of India too undertook a slew of measures to address the issue of both rupee liquidity and forex liquidity. These included, *inter alia*, reduction in CRR in phases from 9.0 percent to 5.5 percent, lowering the Repo rate from 9.0 percent to 6.5 percent, cutting the SLR by one percentage point to 24 percent, enhancing interest rate ceilings on Non-resident (External) Accounts [NR(E)A] and Foreign Currency Non-resident Accounts [FCNR(A)] deposits, relaxing norms for external commercial borrowings (ECBs) and opening a foreign currency swap window for banks.

Central banks in major industrialised economies, by and large, responded with injection of liquidity for a longer period than is usually done. They also resorted to dilution in the quality of collateral required for liquidity support. Most of these operations have not been conducted at the penal rates expected in such situations. This is an unprecedented package which, some observers believe, is indicative of the seriousness of the underlying problems. In addition, there were some specific institution-oriented operations, namely in US, Germany and the UK. While there have been inflationary pressures in most economies, the US has been faced with a threat of serious slowdown in growth warranting a series of cuts in policy rates in recent times.

G-20 Decisions, April 2009: Meeting of the G-20 member countries held on April 2, 2009 in London, decided to undertake a concerted fiscal expansion amounting to US$ 5 trillion to resolve the global crises. They further agreed for over US$ 1 trillion of additional resources for the world economy through international financial institutions and trade finance. It was agreed to treble resources available to the IMF (US$ 750 billion), to support a new SDRs allocation (US$ 250 billion), to support additional lending by the Multilateral Development Banks (at least US$ 100 billion), to ensure support for trade finance (US$ 250 billion), and to use the additional resources from agreed IMF gold sales for concessional finance for the poorest countries.

The G-20 countries additionally pledged to put in place credible exit strategies to ensure long-term fiscal sustainability and price stability. The following major initiatives were agreed upon:

1. Even-handed and independent IMF surveillance of member economies and financial sectors, of the impact of policies on others, and of risks facing the global economy.

2. To establish the much greater consistency and systematic co-operation between countries, and the framework of internationally agreed high standards.

3. Establishment of a new Financial Stability Board (FSB) with a strengthened mandate, as a successor to the Financial Stability Forum (FSF), including all G-20 countries, FSF members, Spain, and the European Commission. The FSB should collaborate with the IMF to provide early warning of macroeconomic and financial risks and the actions needed.

4. Extension of regulation and oversight to all the important financial institutions, instruments and markets including, for the first time, important hedge funds.

5. FSB and the IMF to monitor progress, working with the Financial Action Taskforce and other relevant bodies.

6. IMF to implement the package of quota and voice reforms agreed in April 2008 and complete the next review of quotas by January 2011. For World Bank also, similar reform should be completed on an accelerated timescale, to be agreed by the 2010 Spring Meetings.

7. The G-20 members committed to refrain from raising new barriers to investment or to trade in goods and services, imposing new export restrictions, or implementing WTO inconsistent measures to stimulate exports.

8. The G-20 members should not retreat into financial protectionism, particularly measures that constrain worldwide capital flows, especially to developing countries.

Chiang Mai Initiative: 10 ASEAN members and China, Japan and South Korea have together pledged US$ 120 billion to counter the risk of a currency collapse in the region by enhancing the total size of the multilateralised Chiang Mai Initiative.

Assessment of Damage Control Measures

Governments and central banks around the world have responded to the crisis in an unprecedented show of policy force. The shock and awe of fiscal stimulus and monetary easing is still there. Importantly, given the nature of the crisis, purely national responses have been supplemented by global efforts. At their April 2009 meeting, the G-20 leaders collectively committed to take decisive, coordinated and comprehensive actions to revive growth, restore stability of the financial system, restart the impaired credit markets and rebuild confidence in financial markets and institutions.

The crisis has forced macroeconomic policy around the world into clearly uncharted territory. Governments and central banks have taken unprecedented fiscal and monetary policy measures to prevent the global recession from turning into a protracted depression.

Panic Reaction or Sombre Response: Some experts have opined that this was an over reaction. Others have criticized the tyranny of the short-term compromising medium-term sustainability. However, the mainstream view has been that it is safer to err on doing too much rather than doing too little. Thus, the policy response should be seen as an insurance against this risk. In fact, there is no real way of judging whether it was a panic reaction or sombre response. Broadly speaking, one can say that policymakers all over the world are perhaps erring on the side of over-insuring, i.e. keeping financial markets flush with liquidity and providing substantial fiscal support. They hope to use the breathing space provided by the policy support to restructure the financial system. They also hope that they can withdraw the liquidity and stimulus as the recovery firms up and before inflationary threats take root.

In recent weeks, concerns over inflationary pressures globally have taken the centre-stage even while there are no indications as to whether threats to financial stability have been fully resolved and whether persistent threats of recession in US have abated. Resultantly, the policy dilemmas have become more acute at the current juncture. The most urgent and short-term priority for central bankers at present seems to be to calm the nerves about inflation with an implicit recognition that a somewhat elevated inflation in the short-term may be difficult to avoid.

These acute policy dilemmas between growth and inflation have to be faced in the background of financial turbulence which is yet to calm down. There are also calls for fundamental re-think on macro-economic, monetary and financial sector policies to meet the new challenges and realities, demanding potentially enhanced degree of coordination among monetary authorities and regulators.

Recent measures taken by the governments and central banks do seem to be having a favourable impact on certain segments of the money and credit markets which had faced severe disruptions during the acute phase of the crisis. The policies initiated by central banks and the guarantees offered by governments assuaged to an extent the funding pressures that were evident in the international financial markets during September and October 2008. Despite the host of measures taken in most countries, normalcy continues to elude the international financial markets. This has contributed to the continued uncertainty and deterioration of the world economic outlook. The financial markets need to be stabilised in order to achieve a turnaround in global growth conditions.

Policy Challenges from the Financial Crisis

The challenges faced by developing countries are now compounded by the pressures emanating from the global financial crisis. Policymakers need to respond to the short-term crisis while remaining cognizant of the implications for long-term growth. With policymakers making critical policy decisions on a near daily basis, there is an enormous premium on learning from experience as quickly as possible. Without questions, current circumstances have revealed important weaknesses in crisis preparedness arrangements both within and across countries, including the need for much greater international policy coordination that recognizes the collective character of the crisis and avoids beggar thy neighbour polices.

Major industrial country governments have provided extensive assurances to bank depositors and creditors (and, in a few cases, non-bank financial institutions such as mutual funds) competitive concerns. The scale of these arrangements has no historic parallel. These guarantees would probably be maintained until financial stability is consolidated and credit flows resume on a sustained basis, which may well take several years in some cases.

Some emerging countries are matching these arrangements to prevent capital outflows and/or a shift of deposits to state-owned banks, which are perceived to be safer. However, before moving in this direction, policymakers need to be sure about that the state guaranteed banks—these arrangements are credible, which requires consideration of the state's overall indebtedness and the size of the banking system. That said, given the systemic crisis of confidence, government actions become inevitable and good governance indispensable.

Many of the lessons from the current crisis are equally relevant for both industrial and developing economies. While the crisis has reaffirmed some fundamental tenets of financial sector policymaking, such as the need for a solid financial infrastructure, it is also prompting a reconsideration of several aspects of financial sector regulatory frameworks and supervision. For example, regulators need to ensure that financial innovation does not destabilize financial markets. Overtime, we may see a more fundamental reappraisal of regulation. In particular, there will be new approaches to the scope of regulation (who and what products), greater emphasis on systemic risks (macro-prudential regulations) and an attempt to deal with the pro-cyclical effects of current policies.

Policy Priorities

The financial crisis and the resulting abrupt slowing of global growth occurred as many developing countries have become more vulnerable. Higher commodity prices have raised the current account deficits of many oil-importing countries to worrisome levels (they exceed 10 percent of GDP in about one-third of developing countries) and after having increased substantially, the international reserves of oil-importing developing countries are now declining as a share of their imports. Moreover, inflation is high and fiscal positions have deteriorated both for cyclical reasons and because government spending has increased to alleviate the burden of higher commodity prices.

The countries that are likely to perform better are those that have managed to reduce macro-financial vulnerabilities, increase investment rates, diversify export markets and restore productivity growth. At the same time, a number of developing countries are like to be subjected to substantial strains, until the rapid equity declines and until credit begins to flow again as recent policy actions improve financial market confidence. In these very uncertain circumstances, policymakers must place a premium on reducing the impact on their domestic economies by reacting swiftly and forcefully to emerging difficulties. They must also protect the real sector by taking measures to maintain the flow of short-term and trade credit necessary for economic activity.

The challenge for policymakers is not just to prevent the escalation of the crisis and to mitigate the downturn, but also to ensure a good starting position once the rebound sets in. This means responding rapidly and forcefully to signs of weakness in their financial sectors, including resorting to international assistance where necessary. It also means pursuing a prudent counter-cyclical policy, relying on automatic stabilizers, social safety nets, and infrastructure investments that address bottlenecks that have become binding constraints on long-term sustainable growth. In the current circumstance of heightened risk aversion and investor skittishness, policymakers need to be especially wary of taking on excessive levels of debt or creating the conditions for an inflationary bubble by too aggressive a reaction to the global slowdown. It also means continuing to improve the investment climate for private investment, to increase the flexibility of the private sector to adjust to changing market conditions (business entry and exit) and to generate new jobs and tax revenues.

Protecting the Most Vulnerable

Aid-dependent countries are particularly vulnerable to disbursement shortfalls, changing the donor priorities. Despite recent commitments to improve aid predictability and to scale up official development assistance, progress has been slow and challenges to sustaining these commitments in the current environment are expected to increase. International Development Association (IDA) is in a strong position to assist countries in their pledges to the IDA 15 replenishment in a timely manager. Some donors have raised their already obtained necessary paramilitary approvals and provided written commitments to contribute to IDA 15 and others are striving to complete their ongoing processes as quickly as possible.

At the micro level, even as pressure from high volatile food and fuel prices appears to have begun to abate, the poor will now have to contend with the repercussions of slowing growth. Efforts to expand and improve the targeting of social safety nets, which received renewed impetus and importance under the World Bank's Global Food Crisis Response Program (GFRP) and will also figure prominently in the proposed Energy for the Poor Initiative (EFPI) which the Bank is in the process of discussing with donors, must therefore be sustained. This is particularly crucial if the fiscal impact of a slowing global economy is to be contained. Of the options available, targeted cash transfers tend to succeed best because they have relatively low administrative requirements and minimize the diversion of benefits towards less needy population groups.

However, in countries where there are no targeted programs in place, setting one up from scratch could take four to six toddlers, can be effective; that is especially the case for the distribution of in-kind food aid in fiscally constrained countries. Subsidies, even targeted ones, tend to be much less efficient and costly and be politically difficult to eliminate once introduced. Public works programs rarely provide sufficient coverage to meaningfully target poor families. Whatever policies are adopted, it is critical that the offsetting income support be clearly presented as temporary to avoid creating an unnecessary and unsustainable fiscal burden.

Importance of Multilateral and Coordinated Actions

Multilateral cooperation is essential to address major global challenges and prevent sudden and disorderly market reactions from creating pressure for protectionist and inward-looking policies. The recent situation in food markets has features of a classic "prisoner's dilemma". The introduction of export bans restricted global supply and aggravated shortages. Unilateral actions by exporting countries prompted others to follow suit. Actions by rice importers' who organized large tenders to obtain needed rice imports against a backdrop of shrinking traded supplies, aggravated the problem. It should not be forgotten that many of the distortions that led to the food crisis in the first place can be traced back to the protectionist trade and agricultural policies of rich countries and poorly conceived ethanol subsidies.

Multilateral cooperation is needed if we are to meet the internationally-agreed millennium development goals (MDGs) and ensure inclusive and sustainable globalization. Global coordination efforts must therefore focus on the features of the current situation that are intervention—it is also important to understand the nature and causes of the underlying market failure, the channels through which the proposed remedies will operate, and the consequences both intended and unintended that can result from application of those remedies. Initiatives must balance the need for a blend of short and long-term actions, both at the global and country level, to prevent, mitigate and resolve such crises.

Neither individual governments nor international agencies alone are in a position to offset entirely the costs of financial crisis and high and volatile food and fuel prices. The international community must act in a coordinated and supportive fashion to make each country's task easier. The coordinated provisions of liquidity by major central banks since last year, the additional efforts made more recently, and the decision of the international community to adopt the short-term liquidity facility (SLF) to more quickly mobilize large scale financing from the IMF, are just some examples of how important it is to work together during times of stress in the global economy.

Mutual support must extend beyond the provision of balance of payments financing to encompass areas critical for long-term development and stability. In the wake of the financial crisis, it is imperative that donor countries meet their Gleneagles commitments, reach an agreement on the WTO Doha trade round and follow through on the Bali commitments on climate change. Developing countries must ensure that resources are put to their best and most efficient use, including by putting in place well-targeted social safety nets and improving the targeting of resources provided to the poor.

To sum up, the economic crisis has called into question several fundamental assumptions and beliefs about economic resilience and financial stability. With all the advanced economies—US, Europe and Japan—having firmly gone into recession, global GDP is projected to contract for the first time since the Second World War. The contagion of the crisis from the financial sector to the real sector has been unforgiving and total. It appears that the contractionary forces are strong: demand has slumped, production is plunging, job losses are rising and credit markets remain in seizure. Most worryingly, world trade—the main channel through which the downturn will get transmitted on the way forward—is projected to contract in coming years.

The crisis is forcing countries around the world to test the limits of their fiscal and monetary tools. Policy-making worldwide is in clearly uncharted territory. Governments and central banks across countries have responded to the crisis through big, aggressive and unconventional measures. There is a contentious debate on whether these measures are adequate and appropriate, and when, if at all, they will start to show results.

Index

Index